THEY MET AT CALVARY

THEY MET AT CALVARY

W. E. SANGSTER
M.A., PH.D.

HODDER AND STOUGHTON
LONDON SYDNEY AUCKLAND TORONTO

To
SISTER LILLIE SWEET
Wesley Deaconess
Who lives beneath the Cross

PREFACE

MOST of the commerce of earth and heaven begins at Calvary. There are deep reasons why that must be so. Any book, however unpretentious, which draws people to the sacred hill, and constrains them to think reverently on the solemn events which culminated there, will have its usefulness.

I do not claim for this book that it says anything new. I delight in the thought that it is all old, as old as the Gospels. Indeed, I have been especially careful to ignore the traditions and legends which cluster around the men and women who had a part in the death of Christ, and to deal only with things set down in the Scriptures and what (as it seems to me) can be honestly inferred from them.

Even so, not everyone will agree with what I have said. I do not expect it, and will not be distressed. My honest desire and full aim is that I may provoke others to think again on Calvary, and if I succeed there, I shall be more than repaid for my labour.

My grateful thanks are due to Miss Margaret Gregory for typing the manuscript, and to the Reverends Dr Harold Roberts and Dr J. Alan Kay for reading the typescript and giving me the benefit of their keen minds.

W. E. SANGSTER

Westminster

CONTENTS

CHAPTER ONE

THE TEACHERS WHO HATED HIM

THERE is a wide consensus of opinion that Jesus Christ was the one perfect Man who ever lived. That view is held by some who do not hold, as Christians hold, that He was God on Earth. They look at Him and see only humanity, but humanity higher than it had ever been before or has been since.

How came it that a Being so true, so loving, so perfect, was done to death while still in His early thirties? Surely, it borders on the incredible that the human race had no room for the Noble Soul who lifted humanity higher than it had ever been lifted before.

The incredibility of His execution is not removed because Christians believe that His death and their life are for ever bound together; that, in the mysterious statesmanship of God, this greatest of human crimes has become the greatest of heavenly blessings.

The truth is that men *desired* Christ's death; came to conspire for it; planned and plotted and schemed to bring it about; looked upon Him as a danger, a menace, and a terrible challenge to the things they held most dear.

In working for His death, they did not feel that they were the pawns of any supernatural agency—by which I mean that they felt as free as human beings always do. They had a clear and, to them, a reasonable purpose in mind, when they conspired to cause the death of Jesus Christ, and when they went to work, they found allies who ardently wished the same thing. The machination of many persons and cliques culminated at Calvary. On that green hill, outside the city wall, many paths converged, and strange and unexpected people met at Golgotha.

I want us to inquire together why so many people sought the death of Jesus Christ. I want to be as fair to them as I can; to see what was good (if possible) as well as evil in their motives; to try to understand how the greatest felony in history came about; and to ask if, in this solemn event and these mixed motives, we can see at work the human nature which we wear ourselves, and understand the good and evil in our own soiled souls.

I begin with the Pharisees. They came to desire the death of Jesus Christ and to work for it. 'The Pharisees went out, and straightway ... took counsel against Him, how they might destroy Him.'

Why did *they* want to destroy Him? Who were the Pharisees? How came they into conflict with Jesus Christ? What made them accomplices in the foulest crime ever committed?

I

The Pharisees were religious men. They were, in some ways, the best of their race at that time. They had grown up as a school of thought, and a body of teachers, during the centuries between the Testaments. But for their conserving work, it is possible that the Jews would have been lost in the welter of pagan peoples long before Christ was born at Bethlehem.

In the centuries immediately preceding the birth of Jesus, the noble line of Hebrew prophets had ceased to be. There was no Isaiah, Jeremiah, Amos, or Ezekiel—and the Pharisees, as a body, partly filled the gap which had been left by their absence. They stood, as it were, in the Mosaic and in the prophetic tradition. Jesus said on one occasion: 'The scribes and Pharisees sit on Moses' seat.'

But they were not *priests*—or only very rarely. Nobody could be a priest who was not descended from a priestly family. One was *born* to the priesthood, and the Pharisees were not so born.

The Pharisees were rather teachers and preachers, and the guardians of the law. They ran the schools and the synagogues, and, in a sense, became the conscience of the Hebrew people.

There is no doubt that the average Pharisee was a man of high moral character and burningly sincere. He leaned always to the Puritan side. His herculean efforts to keep the nation uncontaminated by admixture with the Gentile world put an iron strictness into his whole way of life. The Jews, he believed, were God's chosen people. They were separate, and separate by Divine appointment. It was important, he held, that they should remain separate. The Pharisees had taken upon themselves to mark out that line of separation and to guard it with vigilant care. They would not eat with Gentiles. They would not do business with Gentiles, or only when they felt compelled. The idea of inter-marriage with non-Jews was a repugnant horror to them.

The strength and the weakness of the Pharisaic position is seen very plainly in our Lord's Parable of the Publican and the Pharisee who went up to the Temple to pray. The Pharisee said: 'God, I thank Thee that I am not as other men: extortioners, unjust, adulterers . . . or even as this publican. I fast twice in the week. I give tithes of all I possess.' And it was all true. Accuse him of what you will, but not of lying. He was *not* an extortioner. Injustice could not be laid to his charge, nor yet adultery. He fasted twice in the week. (However hearty his appetite, he curbed it on Monday and Thursday with a fast!) He gave tithes of all he possessed. (How many Christians parallel the Pharisees in giving at least a tenth of their income to God?) He subjected himself to as rigorous a code of rules as is known outside iron-asceticism.

It is impossible to withhold some admiration from the Pharisees. Men of this cast of mind are thrown up by the religious conscience in all ages. Puritans do not belong only to the sixteenth century and to England.

They belong to most races and all ages. They are all-out men. They want the highest. No régime is too strict for them. They will fulfil all the law requires . . . and then some more!

We can see this spirit in certain orders of the Roman Church: we see it in the fastings, and in the vigils, and in the self-imposed dumbness, and in the daily solitariness of some monastic orders. We see the same spirit in certain groups of evangelical Christians: they mentally withdraw from the world; they limit their contacts with other people for fear of becoming contaminated. They never exercise their vote.

We see it in the Pharisees.

There is something in this spirit to admire. In an age of compromise, these men will *never* compromise. They are standing by the law as they understand it, and if necessary they will die for it as well.

II

How came these men to get into conflict with Jesus Christ?

That they were in conflict with Him, nobody who reads the New Testament can deny. The Pharisees appear in a very poor light in Matthew, Mark, Luke, and John.

Many Jewish Rabbis seriously resent the picture the New Testament gives of the Pharisees. They say that the Gospels offer a false idea of the Jewish Puritans, and that Christians are ignorant of the high service the Pharisees rendered to their race.

It would be fair to remember that it is possible to say things which are perfectly true concerning other people, and yet, because those things are *selective*, to give an unbalanced picture at the last.

I met a man some time ago who was positively shocked to learn that I was a Methodist. He was unused to Church circles of any kind, but Methodists were his particular aversion.

'*You can't mean it,*' he said with incredulity. 'Not a Methodist! Why,' he went on, 'those are the people who take the working man's pint from him, and his pools. They preach an ugly, repressive creed, and are only heard of in public life when they want to oppose something!'

Now, of course, there is some truth in what he said. *Some!* But, only by selection, the whole picture has become distorted and borders on a caricature.

The Rabbis feel that something like that has happened to the picture of the Pharisees in the New Testament. Because they only appear when they are in controversy with Jesus—and no man can appear to advantage if he is in controversy with Christ—the picture gives no portrait, so the Rabbis think, of their fine qualities. The things said about them may be true, but other things could have been said as well. Many leaders of modern Jewry believe that a fuller account would have given us a kinder picture of the Pharisees than we now possess.

Let us allow something to that view-point, but the question still remains: 'How came this sharp conflict between the Pharisees and the Noblest Son of their race?'

The reasons are both of principle and personality.

1. *In the first place, they were angered by Christ's note of authority.*

Believing what we do about Jesus Christ, we understand the note of authority. He came from God the Father. He spoke from God the Father. He did not temporize, much less compromise. He *announced*. The common people noticed it immediately. They said: 'He teaches as one with authority and not as the scribes.'

But, inevitably, that note of authority offended the Pharisees. As educated men, and leaders of the people, they were wont to receive from the uneducated masses (among whom they placed Jesus) a certain deference and special respect. Jesus gave them neither. He treated them with the kindness and independence with which He treated others, but He did not defer to them in the way that they wished. And they resented that. They began to ask: 'Who is He, anyhow? He's a carpenter from Nazareth. He speaks with a Galilean accent. He has never been properly educated. He has just been to one of our synagogue schools. He never graduated from a scribal college. He never sat at the feet of the Rabbis.'

While they were thinking these things, the voice of the Nazarene was ringing in their ears:

'I am the Bread of Life.'

'No one cometh unto the Father but by Me!'

'I and the Father are One.'

They were angry with our Lord, in the first place, because of that tremendous note of authority.

2. *They were angry, in the second place, with Christ's universalism.*

The Jews were God's chosen people. There are senses in which instructed Gentiles readily concede this even today. They had a spiritual mission to the whole world. But it became a source of great national pride in them, and especially in the Pharisees. They spoke out from the crowds sometimes, and challenged the teaching of Jesus by saying, 'We are children of Abraham,' and He had to make the most trenchant replies to that deep nationalism in them.

He was swift to recognize the half-truth in what they said. He always conceded that it was to the Jews that he had come *first*. Most certainly! Only among them *could* He have been born, and His mission was primarily to them . . . but not to them *only*. The implications of His message were universal. Beginning at Jerusalem, it was to encompass the wide world. No racial inferiorities are compatible with His teaching. People who want to preach doctrines of racial superiority and inferiority must look elsewhere for their authority. It cannot be found in Jesus Christ. He had time for the Samaritan woman at the well. He had time for the Syrophoenician woman also. The coming of the Greeks to Him before the Cross lifted up His shadowed spirit.

The Pharisees were angry with Him because He seemed to deprecate the separateness and spiritual superiority of their race.

3. *They were angry, also, because of Christ's indifference to some aspects of their puritanism.*

Notice that it was only of *some* aspects of their puritanism that Christ was critical. Their fine moral record would have been, in its wholeness, a joy to Jesus. But there were some aspects of their puritanism He could never abide.

If the publicans and sinners had a party and asked Jesus, Jesus went. When Matthew forsook his old life to follow Christ, and gave a farewell feast to his friends, Jesus was there. Sometimes He actually invited Himself. Zacchaeus was the most notorious publican in Jericho, and Jesus, when visiting Jericho, invited Himself to the home of Zacchaeus for a meal.

That was a terrible shock to the Pharisees. Even those among them who believed that He might, indeed, be a prophet of God, were shaken by that. They said in bewilderment one to another: 'He has gone in to one who is a publican and a sinner.'

4. *They were angry with Christ also because of His attacks upon them.*

People whose acquaintance with the New Testament is slight sometimes suppose that Christ never used denunciation. They should read the twenty-third chapter of St Matthew. After all these centuries it burns still. Christ *lashed* the Pharisees. He called them 'hypocrites' to their face. Five times in a few verses He utters His 'woes' upon them. He calls them 'blind guides'. He calls them 'whited sepulchres'.

It is not in human nature to like people who talk about us in that way. The Pharisees were angry with Him because of His terrible attacks on them.

5. *Finally, they were angry at Christ's popularity.*

'The common people heard Him gladly.' In the jargon of today, we could say truly that there were periods in His ministry when He 'got the crowd'.

Perhaps it was this which brought all the animosity of the Pharisees to a head. Intellectuals and purists often affect to despise the masses, but they do not despise them really. At least, if they despise them with one part of their mind, they secretly covet their applause with another.

I have known men—academics usually—who spoke with scorn of the popular newspapers as being beneath the contempt of an educated man, and yet, if their own names got mentioned in those sheets, they seemed quite surprisingly pleased that they were there.

There was something of that in the Pharisees. They half-despised the people, and yet they wanted their applause and approval. If they ever had it, Jesus stole it from them for a while. He seemed able to fascinate even their own servants. They sent their officers one day to arrest Him and bring Him before the council— they were in league with the Sadducees at the time— but the officers came back without Jesus. When they were asked why they had not done their duty, they

could only gape and say: 'Never man so spake.' And
the Pharisees said with bitterness: 'Are you also led
astray?'

Well, there it is! We see there the grounds of their
animosity. They were angered by our Lord's note of
authority, by His universalism, by His indifference to
some forms of their puritanism, by His attacks on
them personally, and by His popularity with the
people.

III

But, even allowing for all that, how did they come to
desire and seek His death? It is one thing heartily to
dislike a man, and to have what you judge to be good
reasons for so doing, but to move from that into
schemes for his execution is to move a long way.

It probably happened like this. If you dislike
people, all your information about them takes the dye
of your dislike. Everything they do, everything you
hear that they do, gets interpreted in your mind in
that biased way.

The very dislike the Pharisees had of our Lord
meant that their reasons for disliking Him became
heightened in colour.

The note of authority they interpreted as blasphemy: 'He puts Himself in the place of God!'

That note of universalism they interpreted as being
traitorous: 'The man isn't loyal to His own race!'

That indifference to certain aspects of their puritanism they took to be morally dangerous: 'This man

associates with publicans and sinners. A man is known by the company he keeps!'

His personal denunciation of them, and His popularity with the people, they talked themselves into regarding as an effort to deceive the masses.

Putting all these things together, they concluded that He was a danger to the nation. He must be destroyed. When they set out to do that, they found themselves with unexpected allies. People they normally disliked were wanting the same thing. It brought them in line with the Herodians, and with the Sadducees, and, at the last, even with Rome. So they went to work. The best men of their age became prime movers in the greatest crime of all history.

IV

What are the things which sincere men and women can learn from all this?

Is this study purely historical, and of interest only because of the light it sheds on the past? Or do these facts point to things we should recognize as dangers to ourselves?

I would stress two things about that.

Keep saying to yourself: '*They were good men.*' The Pharisees present the most terrible illustration in all history of how good people can go wrong. You can be an upholder of the law; you can be a close student of the Book; you can be forward in all things that make for the moral well-being of our race, and yet you can go as terribly and tragically wrong as the Pharisees went. You can crucify the Son of God afresh.

It is usually spiritual pride which ensnares men of
this quality. They reach the dizzy heights of moral
achievement and they forget that one can only live at
those heights upon one's knees. They begin to think
that they themselves are the architects of their own virtues. It was all pictured for us in the Parable of the
Pharisee and the Publican in the Temple. The Pharisee can go up to the Temple and boast of his virtues in
the presence of God, but the publican, who beats his
breast and cries for mercy, goes down justified rather
than the other.

Most people who would have any interest in this
book are probably regarded as 'good' people in their
locality, and many of them are in the Puritan tradition.
In all humility, let us remember before God that, unless our lives are controlled by the Holy Spirit, we also
may go tragically wrong. It is a particular danger of
the good at any time. The Pharisee could take over in
us. We also could be blind guides.

Here is the second thing. Remember, as Paul said
elsewhere: 'The letter kills, but the spirit gives life.' It
is a sad thing when the warm life of God in Jesus is
chilled by the rigour and coldness of our moral codes.
Such things can happen. I have known good men,
men whose word was their bond, who were honest in
all their business dealings, just and above reproach in
the commerce of the nation, and yet strangely lacking
in tenderness and in that melting love we look for in a

follower of Christ.

We stand for strict moral principles, but when the principles we have taught are disregarded, and an unmarried girl comes in penitence to confess that she is to be a mother, let us not spurn her for her sins but stretch out loving hands and help her back to God.

We claim to be firm in moral principle, and we warn people against the peril of hard drink, but when a man, disregarding our counsel, finds himself in the grip of alcoholism, let us be careful not to spurn him in his drunkenness but to keep the fellowship unbroken and lead him back to a disciplined life of self-control.

The Pharisees had lost tenderness. If we lose tenderness we shall be more guilty than they because we have a nobler example.

Let us begin these studies in the humility of those who know that they, also, could go gravely wrong.

CHAPTER TWO

THE PRIESTS WHO BOUGHT HIM

WE have come to the second of 'The Roads That Led to Calvary'. We have now to consider the path the Sadducees took. They also desired the death of Jesus and schemed for it. They actually said it was expedient that he should die. Who were the Sadducees? How did they come into conflict with Jesus? Why did they desire His death? Is it possible that their errors also can be found in us?

I

Nobody knows for sure how the word 'Sadducee' was derived. The majority of scholars think that the term originated in the name of Zadok, a notable priest of the period of David and Solomon, or from a later priest of the same name. Whatever be the truth about that, we know that the party, as a party, took shape some two hundred years before the birth of Christ.

When the Jews returned from exile, they relied very much upon their priests. They had no king. They had no desire for a king. They wanted to be a theocracy more than a monarchy. They wished to be a community ruled over by God and, therefore, through the agency of His priests.

In the early days, the priests deserved both their fame and their influence. They rallied a broken people. They became the aristocracy of Jewry.

No one could belong to the higher order of priests who was not born in a certain family. The high priesthood was a closed corporation, and it suffered from the faults of aristocracy at all times. It was exclusive. It said to the rest of Jewry: 'Only us.' It was stubbornly conservative in its attitude on all public questions, resisted change, and constantly held aloof from contact with the common crowd.

Among the Jews, by the very nature of their community life, politics and religion were not kept apart. The priests were not only the spiritual leaders of the people; they were the statesmen too. Unhappily, as the years went by, the politics prevailed over the spiritualities, and the priesthood, in its upper layers, was composed of men who were completely preoccupied with the conduct of affairs and notoriously self-seeking.

When, in the course of history, Palestine was included in the Roman Empire, it was with the Sadducees that the Romans dealt. Indeed, Rome used these governing priests rather like the Germans used Pétain and Laval and the men of Vichy during the years of occupation in France, during the Second World War. Rome had its procurators over the Jewish provinces, but the procurators were expected to work with the high-priestly party. Rome often allowed a certain freedom of worship to conquered peoples, and it had proved best to rule the Empire, in some areas, through native leaders—a policy which was followed in recent centuries in the British Empire.

The Sadducees became, therefore, the pawns of the Romans. Their own position and security and comfort depended, in part, on their relationship with the Emperor and his officers. Inevitably, this led to a certain subservience and to still more politics rather than religion.

Those, then, were the Sadducees—aristocratic Jews exercising the highest functions of priesthood. Their head was the High Priest himself—Caiaphas, in the time of Jesus. If you could imagine England as an occupied country which was governed under the occupying power by a House of Lords all of whose members were both hereditary and spiritual (a difficult idea to hold in mind), you would get a rough idea of the situation as it existed in the time of our Lord.

II

How came the Sadducees into conflict with Jesus?
There is comparatively little reference to the Sadducees in the Gospels. It is not hard to understand why. The Sadducees were 'high and lifted up'. They were the priestly aristocracy. To them the Man of Nazareth was just a 'hot-gospeller'—so far beneath them that, except on rare occasions, they did not even notice Him. The name 'Sadducee' is only mentioned nine times in the Gospels: seven times in Matthew, once in Mark and once in Luke. It is not mentioned

at all in John. It was with the Pharisee that our Lord
came into conflict from the start. The Sadducee,
throughout His early ministry, barely knew that He
was there.

But they did on occasion, and on one occasion in
particular. It was when our Lord cleansed the
Temple. Jesus arrived at the Temple to find the outer
courts used as a cattle and bird market, and as a place
for the changing of money. The holy place was being
desecrated. Instead of the decent quiet which should
attend God's house, there was the hustle and scurry-
ing and smell and cheating of an oriental bazaar. It
was all done with the permission of the priests, who
had their own 'rake-off' from it. They would have
argued, no doubt, that the law required the sacrifices,
and that it was a convenience to the people to have the
birds and beasts at hand. They would have said, also,
that it was unfitting for the Temple tribute to be paid
in heathen money, and that facilities must be provided
for the visitors to obtain Jewish currency when they
came. They turned a blind eye to the fact that the
poor were fleeced, and they lived in luxury themselves
on their share of the dirty trade.

They could not turn a blind eye, however, to the
action of Jesus. The iniquity and the profanity of their
Temple market so overcame Him that He picked up
some cords and drove the animals and traders out, and
turned over the tables of the money-changers. It is one
of the most terrible examples in Scripture of the
'Anger of the Lamb'. He was a marked man after that.

Even the lofty Sadducees (their pockets being touched) took sinister heed of Him.

One day—how long after the Temple cleansing we can only guess—the High Priest received a messenger from the Pharisees. That, in itself, may have been a little unusual. Contact was not close between them. But the messenger made it clear that the Pharisees would like a little help. There was a dangerous impostor abroad. The High Priest would remember that young fanatic from Galilee who had cleansed the Temple, overturning the tables of the money-changers. He was a blasphemous hot-head and a danger to the nation. The Pharisees would like the co-operation of the priests in getting him out of the way.

Now, it is a fact widely recognized that sin makes strange bed-fellows. Normally, the Pharisees and the Sadducees had little to do with one another. There were important differences between them. The Pharisees were Puritans; the Sadducees were not. The Pharisees were passionately moral; the Sadducees were only mildly moral. The great interest of the Pharisees was religion; the great interest of the Sadducees was politics. The Pharisees were in close touch with the people; the Sadducees were remote from the people. The Pharisees had room for any bright boy, and would educate him in their own order; the Sadducees were exclusive—you could only be born a Sadducee.

Nor were the differences confined to that. They differed in doctrine too. The Pharisees believed in the resurrection of the body; the Sadducees denied it (though they may have had some very vague and shadowy hope of the immortality of the soul). The Pharisees believed in angels and ministering spirits; the Sadducees rejected both. The Pharisees nourished the Messianic hope; the Sadducees had virtually abandoned it.

When you add together all the differences between the Sadducees and the Pharisees—the differences of background, of belief, of manner of life—and when you remember the personal animosity into which these differences often flared up, it is amazing that anything could have drawn these two bodies of men together.

It was a crime which did it, the foulest crime in the human story. The road the Pharisees travelled, and the road the Sadducees travelled, met on a hill outside a city wall. And the name of that hill was Calvary.

III

Why, then, did the Sadducees come to desire the death of Christ? What possible interest could this young provincial preacher have for people so high and mighty as Annas and Caiaphas?

He had grown popular; the people were going after Him in droves. It did not matter where He went; in Galilee, in Perea, and in Judaea, the multitudes flocked around Him.

Amazing stories were told about Him, too. It was said that the sick were healed, that multitudes of hungry people had been fed, that He had raised the dead to life. The Sadducees did not believe it—not for a moment! But the poor, misguided people *did* believe, and that might lead to trouble. The Sadducees concluded that Jesus was one of those recurring nationalist agitators who were not uncommon in Palestine at that period, men eager to lead a revolt of the Jews against the Romans—like Theudas, or Judas of Galilee—and if He got going, well, that would mean trouble with Rome, and more trouble for the people. Four hundred Jews were killed when Theudas revolted. The Sadducees did not want that carnage all over again.

It will be clear, therefore, that the attitude of the Sadducees to our Lord was, as we should expect, more a *political* one than a religious one.

The Pharisees were troubled by what they feared were His political intentions. The Pharisees were troubled by His lack of their kind of Puritanism; the Sadducees were troubled by His ability to lead an insurrection, and His interference with the Temple trade.

So far as the Sadducees were concerned, matters seem to have come to a head after the raising of Lazarus. A man four days in the grave had been summoned from the dead. The Sadducees still did not believe the story, but the people did, and there was no lack of witnesses who said that they had seen the man pulling the grave-clothes off as he came out. The event made such a stir throughout the nation that anything might have happened; multitudes were ready to take a sword and revolt.

Only then did the Sadducees intervene. Only then did they seriously go to work to arrest Him. Only then did Caiaphas utter the phrase that will be for ever famous, the inner meaning of which he could not even conceive himself : 'It is expedient that one man should die for the people.' We need not doubt that there was an element of sincerity in what he said. The Sadducees had persuaded themselves that in putting Jesus to death they would prevent an insurrection, which Rome could easily have crushed, but which would have involved the slaughter of hundreds, and perhaps thousands of their people.

That was how they came into it at all. That was how they got on the road which led to Calvary. That was how

> . . . the deed was done,
> Which shook the earth and veiled the sun.

IV

Is there any particular relevance in this today? Is it just history—history and nothing more?

Three or four things, I think, speak to our need.

The history of the Sadducees shows the absorbing and, at times, the spiritually debilitating character of public affairs. It is not easy for a man to go into the turmoil and compromise of public life and keep his soul. That a number of men do so is a thing for marvel and thankfulness, but no man should face this form of Christian service who is not ready to face also the risks involved.

We greatly desire in the Church of Christ that more and more of our sons shall go into public life in all its forms : into municipal life and parliamentary life, into leadership in their trade unions and in their employers' associations too. We desire it. If Christian men and women fail to serve the community in this way, those who oppose the faith will do it with tragic results.

Yet is is a sad thing, that when men *do* go into public life, religious life is in danger of getting crowded out. Power, place-seeking, honours, seem to take so large a place in their thought and ambition. The Church is often neglected and spiritual values lightly esteemed.

One may recognize, also, in the sins of the Sadducees, the danger which threatens spiritual leaders : that they may become more concerned with their 'church politics' and ecclesiastical machinery than with the souls of the people. Ambition can intrude into any highly organized Church. Place-seeking and hankering do not belong only to lay life. The ordained are not secured by their ordination from a thirst for power and a subtle jockeying for place. God alone knows how much self-seeking is covered with the garments of religion, but any sinful man ought to recognize the danger, and match every 'advancement' that comes to him with more time spent in secret prayer.

It is when ecclesiastics actually assume temporal power that the worst tragedies of all occur. Roman Catholic historians themselves have written of the ghastly iniquities of the Papal States, and no informed Protestant can forget Calvin's major share in burning Michael Servetus. These are instances, like the Sadducees, of ecclesiastics turned statesmen. The world conquered the Spirit in them. Such men are often more bigoted, self-seeking, unyielding, and merciless, than a man without religion at all.

Finally, we should remember from this study of the Sadducees, that we have a special duty to pray for those in authority over us. The exercise of power, especially for the conscientious, is hard, burdensome, responsible, and dangerous. Lord Acton, in an oft-quoted phrase, says that 'power tends to corrupt and absolute power corrupts absolutely'.

We have a duty, therefore, to pray for those who bear office—in Church and State as well. It is laid upon us in the Scriptures. It is laid upon us by a little honest reflection, and a little Christian love. They are bearing great burdens. They could make mistakes with most fearful consequences. They will have much to answer for at the last.

Pray for them!

CHAPTER THREE

THE TRAITOR WHO SOLD HIM

THERE is a terrible sound in the word 'traitor'. A traitor is the very opposite of a loyalist, and the more we love loyalty, the more we loathe a traitor. In this hard world, men expect to be shot at by their enemies, but no one but a cynic expects to be shot at by his friends. And our Lord was no cynic. In all the heaped-up pain of His passion, few things hurt Him more than to be betrayed by one of His own men.

I

To our Lord's pain in His betrayal, we must add a good deal of perplexity in subsequent ages among Christians too. They have found it hard, through the years, really to understand the mind of Judas Iscariot.

It may be that his part in this cosmic tragedy was only a minor one. If mighty forces were bent upon the arrest and death of Jesus Christ, and if Jesus Christ had no intention of resisting their evil will, the part of the man who said, 'I know where He is; I can lead your soldiers there', is not a major one. Soon or late, we may assume, His enemies would have got Him. If Judas had not acted as guide, some other informer outside the apostolic band would have been found.

But the perplexities do not centre chiefly in that.

It perplexes us that anyone who had known Christ with intimacy, who had lived with Him, talked with Him, walked with Him, eaten with Him, and watched Him at work, could do so foul a thing.

It perplexes us, in the second place, that anyone could do so foul a deed for so small a bribe. Thirty pieces of silver! The sum, of course, was not fixed at random. Thirty pieces of silver, as laid down in the Old Testament, was the price of a slave. In the currency of today (it has been calculated), £4.12½. Good God! You wouldn't sell a dog you loved for £4.12½! The reward seems so dreadfully out of proportion to the deed.

It perplexes us, in the third place, because there are passages in Scripture which leave us wondering if Judas was a free agent in this ghastly crime, passages which seem almost to suggest that he was born to do this dire deed and could not escape his destiny.

These are the uncertainties, and not these alone, which have made it so hard for Christians through fifty-seven generations to understand the mind and motives of Judas Iscariot.

II

In an effort to evade these difficulties, some Bible students have been making suggestions concerning Judas which set him in a kindlier light than the Scriptures do, which aim almost at white-washing him, which set out to prove that he was not quite the man he appears to be. These attempts began in early times, but they were popularized in England by De Quincey over a century ago.

I have read them all, I hope, with a reasonably open mind. The chief of these theories run like this:

1. Judas is said by some to have been an honest patriot who had come to the conclusion that Jesus was a danger to the nation; and he betrayed Him, therefore, out of pure love for Israel. What he did, these apologists say, may seem foul to us, but it was the outcome of an honestly mistaken judgement.

2. He is said, by others, to have been a loyal but an *impatient* disciple, completely confident in our Lord's ability to extricate Himself from any situation. Had he not seen a hungry multitude fed with a few loaves? Had he not seen the sick made well and the dead raised up? How could he help but have the supreme confidence in his Lord's capacity to deal with any folk who wanted to arrest Him against His will. And the whole purpose of the betrayal, they argue, was to precipitate the events Judas desired, by putting Jesus in the kind of peril which would compel Him to display His Sovereign power.

3. Still others hold a similar theory, though they express it in a slightly different way. Judas Iscariot, they argue, being in close touch with the people, knew that after Palm Sunday the people were on the very point of insurrection. Unhappily, from his point of view, our Lord seemed at that very moment to become a procrastinator. He did not act as Judas thought He

should. Instead of striding on from the popular acclaim of Palm Sunday to an open announcement of Himself as the King of Israel. He slipped into a kind of retirement, and spent a whole day at Bethany when He should have been among the people, stirring them up. Judas, therefore, brought the soldiers to Gethsemane, these students argue, so that Jesus might be forced to end His procrastination and step out as the King of Glory; and though Judas was wrong there, he was wrong in judgement but not wrong in heart.

4. Finally, there are those who argue that Judas was wavering in his conviction of the Messiahship of our Lord. At moments he was sure; at other moments he was quite unsure. He remembered the wonders Jesus had done, but then he remembered also what the Pharisees and Sadducees were saying about Him, and the question that shaped itself in his mind was this: 'Is He the Messiah or not?'

How could that question be resolved? Judas came to believe that it could be resolved in only one way. Let Him be put to a test. Let Him be arrested on a capital charge, and then, if He was the Messiah, all His mighty power would flash out, and He would be seen as such; and if He was not the Messiah, then He was a terrible impostor and deserved what He got.

Those, I think, are the major efforts that have been made—with a good deal of variation—to explain the perplexities concerning Judas Iscariot which have troubled Bible students for centuries. I find them, frankly, more ingenious than convincing. I believe that many of them are the fruit of a desire in preachers to say something new rather than to say something true. The impressive objection to them all is this: each one of them, on major points, runs counter to the Scriptures.

We know nothing about Judas Iscariot outside the Gospels. If we are to understand and interpret his character, we must sit close to the evidence as we have it. We may find things difficult to explain and inferences unpleasant to draw, but to escape from those difficulties by scorning the evidence is not serious exposition. It is doing violence to the Word of God.

Let us look, then, at some of the facts concerning Judas Iscariot which are laid down in Holy Scripture. John says: 'He was a thief.' Luke says: 'Satan entered into him.' Jesus says: 'It would have been better for him if he had never been born.' Pleasing as it is that Christian preaching should be eager to say the kindest thing it can about the world's most famous traitor, we must, nonetheless, keep to the evidence, and one part of the evidence, alas, is in these sayings. Whatever conclusions we draw must be in harmony with the Scriptures. What was the truth about Judas Iscariot? Basing ourselves on the Bible, what picture do we have at the last?

III

Notice, in the first place, that Judas Iscariot was the only Judaean in the apostolic band. All the others were Galileans. Observe that. It is not unimportant. Of the twelve men Jesus chose 'that they might be with Him', eleven of them came from the north of the country, and one from the south. The southerner was Judas Iscariot. He spoke with a different accent. It is possible that he felt a little bit on his own from the start.

Notice also that he was a man of some commercial acumen. So it seems; for our Lord appointed him their accountant, the keeper of the bag. Their company, as it moved from place to place, was a company of thirteen. (That is probably the origin of the superstition concerning the number thirteen. Thirteen sat down to the Last Supper, and one of them was a traitor. Superstitious people have dreaded the number thirteen ever since.)

When a company of that size moves from place to place, it is better for one person to handle expenses; it saves trouble for the company and for the folk they are dealing with. Judas Iscariot was that man. He had business ability and our Lord made use of it.

It is impossible for us to believe that our Lord chose Judas *in order that he might betray Him*. That does not harmonize with the character of Jesus. If you believe that our Lord's incarnation involved some lack of knowledge (and we remember that there were things He Himself confessed He did not know, and that He expressed surprise on a number of occasions) then it will present no difficulty to your mind that He chose Judas Iscariot with the same affection as He chose the others, and trusted him in a position of responsibility.

If, on the other hand, you believe that our Lord carried long foreknowledge of all these events (and that John 6^{64} means that Jesus knew the destiny of Judas from the beginning of His ministry), you will still remember that foreknowledge is not the same thing as fore-ordination. I know that the sun will rise tomorrow morning, but my knowing it does not make it rise. And it was at least possible for our Lord to know that Judas Iscariot would betray Him, without the knowledge compelling Judas to act as he did. He still acted for reasons of his own and with as much freedom as we human beings ever enjoy.

The painful truth appears to be that Judas Iscariot was a covetous man, that avarice was his sin. We are told that he had been pilfering in the bag some time before there was any talk of his betraying our Lord; the accountant had turned embezzler. He could even hide his greed under the cloak of piety. When Mary of Bethany brought that pound of spikenard ointment and anointed the feet of Jesus, Judas Iscariot was the only one who could not see the inwardness and love of it all. He said, as though he had been shocked by the extravagance: 'Why was not this ointment sold for three hundred pence and given to the poor?'

How pious it sounds!

But John tells us that he did not really care for the poor. If the price of the ointment had gone into the bag which he was keeping, there would have been a little more for him to pilfer. Our Lord, with the shadow of the Cross upon Him, said: 'Suffer her to keep it against the day of My burying, for the poor ye have always with you, but Me ye have not always.'

After Palm Sunday, and when Jesus began plainly to disappoint the hopes of His disciples of an earthly kingdom, Judas Iscariot, as I sadly believe, came to the concluson that there was nothing in this Jesus business—no money, anyhow. It was all a farce. He had thought, when he left his village and joined with the rest of them, that this was going to lead on to fame and fortune. The only outcome of it that he could see now was no fortune and a good deal of infamy. However, he could make a bit out of it. Not much! Thirty pieces of silver. So he went to the High Priest and made the deal.

Perhaps it did not work out just as he had expected. Maybe he only promised at first to take them to the Garden and thought that the soldiers could do the rest; but as they drew near, they saw a cluster of people together, and the soldiers did not know which one of the group to take. Judas had to help them again —even more perhaps than he wished. He said: 'The One whom I kiss is He.' He went forward therefore— was ever the symbol of love so utterly prostituted?— and kissed Him into their arms.

'So they took Him away.'

We all know the terrible remorse that broke over

Judas Iscariot later. Did it come to him immediately? When he saw our Lord suffer arrest meekly, and permit them to march Him off, did the great horror leap up at once in his soul?

It seems that he followed his Master and may have waited outside the Hall of the Sanhedrin during the farce of a 'trial'. As the chief priests were leaving the Hall of Hewn Stone, Judas stopped them, holding the money still in his hands. 'I have sinned,' he cried, 'in that I have betrayed innocent blood.' But they passed on, spurning him. He had played his unimportant part and to them he mattered no more. He ran after them, and before the door of the sanctuary completely closed, he hurled the coins at their backs. Then, with a rope in his hands, he disappeared into the dark.

IV

Does the story of Judas Iscariot speak in any way to our own need?

We learn from it, I think, that it is possible to live near to Christ and then to fall away. We learn that it is possible to be in His company, and be regarded as one of His intimates, and then to be guilty of the foulest betrayal. If any man, in some place of security, asserts in self-confidence that 'nothing could happen to me here', that man has added, by his over-confidence, to the danger we mortals are always in.

I never go to Aber Falls in North Wales, without feeling the pathos of something that occurred there years ago. A brilliant young barrister was climbing the mountain near Aber Falls with a friend. His friend noticed the green slime on the rocks as they climbed and called out: 'Do be careful,' to which young Mr Payne replied: 'Oh, it's as safe as anything. I *couldn't* fall here.' They were the last words he uttered. I know the spot at the bottom of the Falls where his mangled body was picked up.

We may infer, in the second place, that it is possible to be in the Church of God and yet not be a disciple in heart. Was Judas ever a disciple in heart? Who can answer that question? Did he respond, in the first place, out of a deep and sincere devotion to our Lord and fall away in His company, or did he begin with low motives and never capitulate to Him in heart?

No one can answer that question concerning Judas Iscariot, but it is not to be doubted that people can be in the Church without any serious commitment to Christ in their heart. Indeed, their lack of loyalty can be concealed almost from themselves. Until some severe test comes, they are like everybody else. But a trial comes and they are revealed. Some folk have professed allegiance to our Lord and His Church, but when a chance of earthly advancement has presented itself, they have turned their back on Him and the things for which He stands, and taken the chance. Every Christian should periodically question his own soul: 'Am I really in this because of devotion to my Lord? Would I stand if a crucial test came?'

There is a third thing to bear in mind. With some

natures there is nothing so holy that money cannot besmirch it. Watch money. It is so enormously useful and so terribly dangerous. The Bible does not say that money is the root of all evil, but it does say that the love of money is the root of all evil.

Finally, we may learn from the sad story of Judas, how wrong it is ever to limit our Lord's forgiveness. After the betrayal, Judas took his own life. He forgot his betrayed Master's message of forgiveness. Perhaps he was not listening when Jesus said that the love of God was so mighty that it would always meet penitence with pardon. Perhaps he was wondering whether there was enough in the bag to take a little more!

But knowing what *you* know of the forgiveness of God, do you think that if Judas Iscariot had gone, not to hang himself, but to the Cross, and flung himself before our dying Lord and said, 'Lord Jesus, forgive me'—if he had done that, do you think that He who prayed for His murderers as they nailed Him to the wood, and who said to the dying thief, 'Today thou shalt be with me in paradise', that that same Saviour would have refused forgiveness to the man who had kissed Him into their arms?

I cannot believe it. It was the crowning error of Judas's miserable life.

Do not add that sin to any others you may have committed. Do not be like the man with whom I wrestled to a late hour, who, having reviewed the enormities of his past, denied that God would forgive him, and went out, as Judas went out into the night, with the mark of Cain on him and without faith that God would ever wipe it away.

Put no limit to the grace of God!

CHAPTER FOUR

THE CROWD WHO CRIED 'CRUCIFY HIM!'

BIBLE students have long discussed what responsibility the crowd had for the Cross. We know the part the Pharisees played, and the priests, and Judas. But what was the part of the crowd? Were they as guilty as the rest? Did democracy do Jesus to death as plainly as the professional and priestly classes, and would it be true to say that the crowd was as guilty as any other section of the community for the crime of Calvary?

Some students say 'Yes'. They say that it was a fickle crowd—as fickle as crowds always are. They had followed Him on Palm Sunday, and preceded Him as well, thrilled at the thought that the Messiah had come at last. But when nothing happened, they turned on Him; and when Pilate asked them, from the veranda of the Praetorium, 'What, then, shall I do with Jesus who is called Christ?' they cried: 'Crucify Him!' The crowd, say these students, were as guilty as the rest.

Other biblical scholars say 'No'. It was not the *same* crowd which cheered and sneered. The people who followed Him on Palm Sunday were the open-hearted, simple folk, largely drawn from Galilee and other country areas—people whom He never lost, and who were in their beds when the rabble was crying 'Crucify Him!'

Remember the hour. It seems clear that it was very early in the morning when Pilate showed Jesus to the people and invited their judgement.

Remember the place. I can recall my own astonishment when I first saw the space outside what is believed to have been the Praetorium in Jerusalem. I had always had a picture in my mind of a great open space, something like Trafalgar Square in London, or Times Square in New York, and Jesus being brought to the veranda of a Praetorium that was like the arcaded front of the National Gallery, and a great howling mob screaming for His death.

In point of fact, the space at the time was hardly wider than a narrow street. In so confined a space, a hundred people would have made a multitude. The scholars, therefore, who feel that the crowd was not as guilty as it sometimes supposed, say this : 'The people who were there at that hour in the morning were just the sweepings of the slums of Jerusalem, priest-ridden and priest-paid. They were there because they had been told to be there and told what to say. They were suborned. What they did was the result of demagogy at its worst. The priests and their minions had got among them and said, 'Come along. Cry out, "Crucify Him! Crucify Him!" '—and when the Prince of Glory was brought to the veranda they screamed for

His blood.

'Therefore,' say these students, 'it is unjust to say that the crowd turned on Jesus, or to charge democracy with complicity in the crime of Calvary.'

I think the case of those who defend the people is strong. It is hard to believe that the same people who had seen Jesus heal the sick, and give sight to the blind, and preach to the poor, and do a thousand merciful things, could really have shouted with one voice: 'Crucify Him!'

And yet He was crucified. Had the people no responsibility? Was the blame entirely with their rulers? What culpability has a people at any time for the deed of those who rule them? Or should we exempt them and say, 'After all, it was *not* the people'?

This question is not one of merely academic and biblical interest. It is one of the burning questions of recent history and all modern life.

Think back to post-war Germany. One of the most torturing questions then was: 'What responsibility had the ordinary people in Germany for the crimes committed by their rulers? Were they as responsible as those over them? Or were they not responsible at all? Or was it half and half? Think of the persecution of the Jews—the multitudes sent to the crematoria. Think of the atrocities proved beyond all doubting—the horrors of Belsen and Buchenwald. Think of the blood-bath by which the Nazis came to power. (They never denied that they shot hundreds of their own fellow-countrymen in their beds and without even the mockery of a trial.)

When the fighting was over, in an effort to understand the mentality of the German people, the American authorities issued a questionnaire in one of the areas they occupied, and in conditions of absolute secrecy, asked a hundred and fifty typical Germans to answer a set of questions. They wanted to know what the people were thinking.

One of the questions was this:

Who do you think was responsible for the outbreak of war:

1. The German High Command?
2. The Nazi Party Leaders?
3. The German people as a whole?
4. The Allies?

The people had, therefore, a choice of four.

Out of 145 answers:

    20 said 'The German High Command'.

   123 said 'The Nazi Party Leaders'.

     1 said 'The German people as a whole'.

     1 said 'The Allies'.

Notice what the individual people were saying: *'Not me! Not me!'*

The crowd would have said exactly that on the morning after the Crucifixion: 'Not me!'

What is the truth? Were the common people innocent of the crime of Calvary, or does an honest examination implicate them as well?

I

I want to lay it down first that *the ordinary people are powerful*—the ordinary people!

I reject the implication of the constantly reiterated and rhetorical question: 'What can the ordinary people do?' I believe that there is a disparagement and a falsity in it against which thoughtful people should be in constant conflict.

Study the New Testament. We are plainly told that the priestly classes, in their bitter animosities towards Jesus, would have ended His career sooner than they did, except that 'they feared the people'. Notice that. They did not do what they wanted as early as they wanted because '*they feared the people*'.

Notice again. The evangelist tells us that Pilate gave the judgement that he did—having already made up his own mind that the prisoner was innocent—because he was '*willing to content the people*'. Feeling in a cleft stick himself, and groping for something to justify the wickedness of condemning an innocent man, he was only too ready to assume that the early morning company outside the Praetorium was a true cross-section of the people, and that he was yielding to public demand in handing Jesus over as a popularly execrated malefactor.

All history—or nearly all history—shows at some level or other a sensitivity on the part of rulers to the wishes of the people. If it were not so, why should they take so much trouble to mislead and hoodwink them? What is the point of organized propaganda, unless it is to get the people to think what their rulers want them to think? The tyrants who have openly said that they did not care what the people thought (and have acted on those principles) have been short-lived. The ordinary people are more powerful than they know.

If one wanted to take another illustration from British history, one could recall that morning on which the people of Britain opened their newspapers and discovered the terms of the Hoare–Laval Treaty. France and Britain were preparing to agree that Ethiopia should be carved up, and part of it handed over to Mussolini. Most British people were perplexed at that time about the relationships of Italy and Abyssinia, but they were appalled to discover that a British Foreign Minister had made himself a party to dividing up the spoils of the innocent and handing them over to the aggressor. A howl of wrath went up from the country. The ordinary people said, 'The infamy of it!' and within hours the Foreign Secretary was swept out of office.

You see, there are so many ordinary people, and when they act in unity they are more powerful than they know. Lincoln's historic dictum has never been lived. The ordinary people are more powerful than disproved: 'You can fool all the people some of the time, and some of the people all of the time, but you can not fool all the people all the time.'

II

I want, in the second place, to remind you that though the ordinary people are powerful, *the ordinary people are largely indifferent.*

There is a moral inertia in the mass of men which it is almost impossible to move. They are careless about things. They do not want to be bothered.

Somebody hot with indignation on some great moral issue comes into a group of ordinary people and pours out his soul on the subject. For a moment they are impressed, but the impression is evanescent. In the passing of a few minutes, they murmur something about its being 'very unpleasant and all that', and then one of the company (in order to change the subject) inquiries, 'What's on television tonight?'—and that is often the end of it. The great achievement of men like Wilberforce in the task of slave emancipation, and of John Howard in prison reform, was that they toiled on in the face of an awful inertia, and by their own unflagging zeal and tireless persistence made men do the things which, in their best moments, they knew they ought to do. It is not enough to be convinced that something is wrong. The harder task is to convince others of it, and to make them so sure and so indignant that they will do something about it, even at great personal cost.

The ordinary people of this country are not against Jesus Christ. It is fairly easy to get a cheer for Him in the open air. One can quote Him to the mass of people almost anywhere and be heard with respect. Organized and militant opposition to His way of life has never succeeded in Britain. The Rationalist Press Association launched a campaign to raise their membership to 5,000! The membership was to include folk abroad as well as in Great Britain—and at that time there were nearly fifty million people in Great Britain alone. The disparity of numbers was ludicrous. There are more devout and recognized believers in Jesus Christ in one small town than the 'rationalists' can register in the whole country.

But though the people of this land are not against Jesus Christ, and indeed at some level of their mental life they have a deep respect for His Person and His teaching, they are inert. They are not willing to toil and sacrifice for the things He is seeking. The crowd which will cheer Him at one moment will disperse at the next if the speaker challenges its members to take up a cross and follow Him.

There is the pain of the situation, and there is the obdurate impediment to spiritual progress—not in the opposition of the people, but in their awful indifference.

III

Notice in the third place that the *ordinary people under democracy can have whatever they want.*

'Democracy' is a word sometimes loosely and even falsely used; it has been employed to cover subtle forms of autocracy and bureaucracy. But real democracy, when it is honestly practised, is a precious thing. Not without great sacrifice from men and women of the past has democracy been achieved. Universal adult suffrage! Freedom of speech and discussion! Secret ballots! People who have always enjoyed these privileges seldom realize how great they are.

Under democracy the ordinary people can have whatever they want.

But they must want it passionately enough. Their passion must weld them into unity, and gird them with courage, and toughen them to a terrible persistence.

So far as effective action is concerned, to be neutral or indifferent on a moral issue is indistinguishable from a vote against it. That is how a handful of vigilant, passionate zealots can capture and run a vast trade union, made up for the most part of men who are against the ultimate aims of the zealots, but whose laziness and indifference opens the door to the dynamism and subtlety of the people who manage the machine.

I am in no doubt that the mass of ordinary people, who had seen Jesus work wonders and who loved Him well, were unspeakably distressed by His crucifixion; but when the deed was done they were in bed. His enemies worked swiftly in the early hours of that solemn day which divides all history. When the ordinary folk were astir and about, He was already on the cross. Many of them, no doubt, were shocked. They could have protested, with a good deal of cogency, that they were not to blame.

It is hard to blame people for not being vigilant, harder still for not being heroes. But that is how wickedness wins its way in this world. It counts on the sleepiness and comfort-loving character of the good— and it wins.

When the last war ended, I had a great longing to meet my old Christian friends in Germany. For the most part, they belonged neither to the valiant group which Hitler had found it necessary to put in prison, nor yet to those evil men who called themselves 'German Christians' and had become the willing tools of Nazi wickedness. They belonged to the large central body of Christian people who had somehow been 'by-passed' in Hitler's rise to power.

At last the time came, and we were face to face. I asked my questions and they heard them with embarrassment. Many of them told me that they had no idea there were such places as concentration camps. No idea! Others said that they had heard nothing of the extent and wickedness of Jewish persecution. They had been aware of some minor anti-Semitism (which they half-regretted and half-excused), but of the wholesale slaughter of decent people on the grounds of their race, they knew nothing.

Then they added other things :

'It isn't good for Christians to get mixed up in politics.'

'We had been partly persuaded that National Socialism was good for Germany.'

'We had only the newspapers really to go on, and we did not realize how much they were controlled.'

'We thought that Martin Niemöller was being a little wooden and unco-operative.'

So it was done. The good people had been fooled—to their own awful cost, and to the awful cost of half the world.

Were the people responsible for the crime of Calvary?

Not, I think, in the way which some scholars have supposed. Not with malice aforethought; not with a diabolically thought-out judgement given against Jesus.

They were guilty by inertia, guilty as we are guilty today—guilty of moral torpor, and of being so self-obsessed and comfort-loving that we will not stir ourselves and suffer for the truth.

On those counts the people were guilty then, and on those counts most of us are guilty now.

CHAPTER FIVE

THE JUDGE WHO SENTENCED HIM

To use the world 'trial' of the judicial proceedings which culminated in the crucifixion of Jesus Christ is to mis-apply a good term. It seems that eight hours after His arrest He was on the Cross. In the brief space of six hours He was examined five times and by four different authorities. He was accused by witnesses who contradicted themselves, condemned on a deliberate misinterpretation of His words, and sentenced by a judge convinced of His innocence. Yet this can never rob the record of moving power. The issues involved are so tremendous, the characters are so clearly etched and vivid, and the consequences are so momentous for the whole human race.

Prominent in the last scenes is Pontius Pilate, the Roman Procurator of Judaea, to the study of whose character we must now turn.

We have three sources of information concerning this man: the writings of the Jewish historian Josephus, the works of Eusebius, an early Church Father, and the Gospels. Of these, the works of Eusebius are more legendary than historical, and for our purpose can be disregarded. Josephus gives the history of Pilate's appointment and rule, while the Gospels shed a searching light on his inner character. The combina-

tion of these two sources provides a picture clear and
arresting.

Of Pilate's ancestry, nothing is known. He was a
Roman of equestrian rank – a man of the 'middle
classes', as we might say today. His position in Judaea
was that of a Procurator—sub-governor under the
Governor who ruled all Syria. In itself it was not a
high position, but was often sought as a stepping-
stone to bigger things. The Roman law forbad the appointment to this office of anyone under twenty-seven
years of age. Pilate was appointed in the year A.D. 26
and could not therefore have been less than thirty-one
at the time of the crucifixion of Christ. How much
older he was, it is impossible to say.

His association with the Jews was unhappy from the
first. They were a difficult people for anyone to govern, but particularly for a junior official of limited experience. In accordance with their universal custom,
the Romans had given the Jews full religious freedom,
and in one particular had been especially conciliatory
and granted them an unusual concession. Judaism, as
is well known, was the only important religion of the
Old World completely intolerant of idols, and at this
time Emperor worship was being fostered among the
Roman legions. The Roman soldiers were being encouraged not only to recognize their Emperor as king,
but to worship him as God, and accordingly they carried about on their standards little images to which
they offered adoration.

Now the special privilege granted the Jews was just

this: it was agreed that these idols should not be used in the vicinity of their holy place; no image was to be brought to the precincts of the Temple.

Pilate arrived in Judaea and, almost at once, scornfully disregarded this concession. He sent his garrison troops to Jerusalem to winter, and ordered that the standards, with the idolatrous images upon them, should be taken by night into the sacred city. The Jews awoke next morning to discover the vile things under the shadow of their Temple. Their religious sentiment was outraged. Multitudes of them marched all the way from Jerusalem to Caesarea (where the Procurator normally lived) and pleaded for an interview. For five days Pilate would not see them, but on the sixth he admitted them to his presence, and they begged him on their knees to remove the hateful things.

The Roman never fully understood this fierce intolerance of the Jew.

Suddenly, in the midst of their pleading, Pilate ordered his troops to surround them, and threatened them with instant death if they persisted in their request. To his utter amazement, they stretched themselves on the ground to a man and declared that death was better than the violation of their laws. Pilate was beaten. Even a Roman Procurator could not indulge in wholesale massacre. He granted their request and let them go.

In his next important difference with them he had a little more success. Pilate decided to build an aqueduct to Jerusalem, and for this purpose took the contents of the Temple Treasury. The Jews were bitterly resentful. Pilate's purpose in building the aqueduct has been the subject of sharp controversy. It has been argued, on the one hand, that he had the real interest of the Jews at heart. Water was never plentiful in the capital, and at feast times it was perilously low. It is said that it was for their national well-being that he undertook the work, and consequently they should have borne the cost. On the other hand, it has been argued that he had no unselfish motives in mind. Pilate knew that if ever the Romans had cause to lay siege to Jerusalem (which actually happened forty-one years later), their ultimate victory would be long delayed by the absence of an adequate water supply. It was for this reason, it is said, that the aqueduct was built, and the Jews ought not to have paid for it.

It is impossible to decide, after this lapse of time, which explanation is correct, but in any case the outcome was the same. The Jews were indignant. They argued that they paid their imperial tribute in the usual ways; it was not within the province of any Roman official to appropriate money which they had given to their God. Riots broke out all over Jerusalem.

Pilate acted swiftly and effectively. He filled the city with soldiers disguised as peasants and armed with clubs, and order was restored very soon. What Pilate could *not* restore (because it had never existed) was a kindly feeling between himself and the people he governed. The smouldering flame of resentment in Jewish hearts steadily increased, and even when they fawned on him, it was only a cover for an ever-deepening hate.

And now Pilate became aware of danger from another source. The Roman Emperor at this time was Tiberias, who, despite his later corruption, commenced his reign with singular prudence and overlooked the administration of the provinces with meticulous care. To the ears of Tiberias had come rumours and complaints concerning Pilate's relation with his people. There is some evidence that the Emperor had actually received from the Jews written protests against the methods of the Procurator, and Pilate seems to have received warning that he must amend his ways. Further complaints, it was hinted, would endanger not only his future prospects but his immediate standing.

This is the background against which we must view the condemnation of Christ. Now we are in a position closely to examine the character of the man who placed the official seal on the crime which stains all history.

The four evangelists have but one purpose in writing their Gospels—to tell the story of Jesus Christ. Other characters are incidental; they are of importance only in the measure in which they touch Him, but as they touch Him they get their valuation. He seems to move through the story like some unconscious Assessor, some Touchstone, whereby the real worth of men is revealed and their innermost nature made clear. We never seem to see a man until he is appearing in the same scene as Jesus. It is when he moves in the direct beams of the Light of the World that we are no longer deceived by the tinsel of earth—whether he be High Priest or Procurator—and we see him *as he is*.

So let us look at Pilate.

II

Pilate was a Roman. That is not a trite statement; it has to be borne in mind all the time. He belonged to the world conquerors, almost to a superior order of beings. He had all the overbearing arrogance of his race, added to a deep-rooted contempt for the people he governed. He replies to a question of our Lord's by asking: 'Am I a Jew?' Pilate would have regarded the imputation of Jewish nationality as the greatest insult you could offer him. He never understood his subjects. It is doubtful if he ever tried to understand them. He would have said it was not his business to understand; it was his business to govern.

He was a cynic. Cynicism is usually the product of culture without real religion. It is what we should expect of such a man in such an age. He knew something of the subtle intrigues of the imperial court; he knew that influence more than merit secured the coveted appointments; he had seen honest men fail and rogues succeed; and he had no antidote for all that dirty chicanery.

There is only one antidote: a strong religious conviction. And for religion, Rome provided a voluptuous paganism; Christ's hour had not yet come. Under cross-examination, Jesus asserted that He came into the world to bear witness to the Truth, and Pilate cynically inquired: 'What is Truth?'

Yet like most cynics, and men generally who seek to crush the impulse to religion in them, he was not free from superstition. He was strangely disquieted by the sublime dignity of Christ. There was an air of detachment about his prisoner, a nobility, almost a superiority, which he found disturbing.

Pilate was annoyed—annoyed with himself for not finding it easy to condemn a Jew, annoyed with Jesus that He was not impressed with Pilate's presence. 'Speakest thou not unto me?' he asks. 'Knowest thou not that I have power to crucify Thee and have power to relase Thee?' He moves between the clamant Jews outside the Praetorium and the silent prisoner within, and a superstitious fear grows in his heart. He does not believe the charges; they are lies. He is familiar enough with the typical rebel, and knows very well that this man is no 'perverter of the nation' or serious rival of Caesar. Meanwhile a messenger arrives from Pilate's wife urging him to release the prisoner, as she 'has suffered many things in a dream because of Him', and Pilate's perplexity increases. John says: 'He was the more afraid and from thenceforth sought to release Him.'

Let this little be said to his credit—he did endeavour feebly to administer justice. When they first brought their unresisting captive to him, he refused to hear them except on a stated political charge. When he had examined the prisoner, and assured himself of His innocence, he stated that fact definitely before them all. When this failed to get them to withdraw the charges, he seized on their own custom and offered Jesus as the prisoner who should be released at the feast. But to this the Jews replied with their last and strongest argument: 'If thou let this man go thou art not Caesar's friend; whosoever makes himself a king speaks against Caesar.' Their case was won then. The fierce struggle in the mind of Pilate was over. Superstitious fear, the good in him, and his sense of justice on the one side, stood opposed to private ambition and his sense of security on the other; and the selfish element won. He could not risk further complications at Rome. Deliberately, he condemned an innocent man to death.

The judgement of history on Pilate has varied widely. Philo, on the one hand, denounces him as an unmitigated scoundrel, and the Coptic Church, on the other, believing the legend of his conversion, reveres him as a martyr and a saint. Both are exaggerations. He is, like most of us, between the two. His central weakness was here: the good in him was unbuttressed by moral principles; he preferred his social standing to any spiritual stability. He would not be a just man, if to be a just man, he must be a poor man. Moral values clashed with earthly values—and he chose the earthly.

This is where our likeness to Pilate grows more apparent. We must all face this issue sooner or later. To every man and woman the inevitable choice comes. Indeed, it is coming constantly. 'Which is first in my

life—the spiritual or the material?' We know that
within ourselves there are two warring elements.
There are the higher aspirations of our soul, and the
lower, coarser tendencies of our nature. We are constantly legislating between the two. Our best self
points out the hard and costly way; our lower self de-
rides it and urges us to 'play for safety'. Our best self
challenges us to be the highest we have power to be;
our lower self tells us that we must always take care of
'number one'. So the struggle goes on. So our essential character is shaped. The light of eternity will re-
veal what we have become.

Pilate pronounced sentence and then took water
and washed his hands saying: 'I am innocent of the
blood of this just person.' He washed his hands, but
the blood-guiltiness was on his soul. How often in the
history of the world men have deluded themselves into
believing that some external rite was efficacious to remove sin! How often men have compromised with
evil, sold themselves for the wares of this world, and
sought to dope their accusing conscience by giving a
fragment of the price to charity. Micah settled that
question twenty-seven centuries ago: 'Will the Lord
be pleased with thousands of rams, or with ten thousands of rivers of oil? . . . What doth the Lord require
of thee, but to do justly, and to love mercy, and to
walk humbly with thy God?'
Pilate returned from the Praetorium, doubtless, to
the remonstrances of his wife. He had condemned a

just man despite her plea. One can almost hear him
testily replying: 'Yes! Yes! I know! Yes! Of course
—but it's done now, and it will be all over and forgotten in a fortnight.' All over and forgotten in a fortnight! And for two thousand years, in ever increasing
volume, from north, south, east, and west, from tiny
Bethel and mighty cathedral, the incessant murder has
arisen ... 'Born of the Virgin Mary, *Suffered under
Pontius Pilate*, was crucified, dead, and buried...'
Was ever retribution more complete and persistent?
He fell from power almost immediately through
trouble with the Samaritans, was recalled to Rome,
and disappears from history. The legends about him
are legion—but they are only legends.

His fault at heart was such a common one. He
would not be loyal to the highest that he knew, when
to be loyal was costly. He would not maintain such
moral integrity as he had if its maintenance threatened
to involve him in personal loss.

There is something of that weakness in all men.

You. Me.

There is something of the *guilt* of it in millions.

It proves again that Christ was not crucified by a
few sins of rare vileness, but by a multitude of common sins of which we are all guilty.

> *Oh Jesus, my hope,*
> *For me offered up,*
> Who with Clamour pursued Thee to Calvary's
> top ...

CHAPTER SIX

THE THIEVES WHO DIED WITH HIM

JESUS CHRIST did not die alone. One Cross always stands out in our memory and in the history of the world, but it would not have seemed like that to a casual spectator on the first Good Friday morning. Crucifixion was a common form of execution then. Any visitor to Jerusalem, passing the Place of the Skull on that never-to-be-forgotten day, might have remarked when he got to his lodgings : 'I saw three men crucified today.'

Three men! Three crosses! How similar they were in some ways!—their agonized bodies sagging on the pierced hands, the raging thirst that tortured them in the dust and heat, the naked spectacle for all to gaze upon. The same for all three!

I wonder what led the rulers to crucify Him with thieves? Was it just 'an accident', as some might say? Did the captain of the execution squad remark to his men : 'There are two others under sentence. Better make a job of it. Do all three of them together?' Or was it another refinement of cruelty thought out by His enemies?—a calculated detail added to heighten the shame; to stress, if they could, His criminal character? 'A man is known by the company he keeps'!

Crucify Him with thieves. Ha! Ha! Ha!'

I do not know. I know this. He did not die alone.
There were three. The crosses were the same and the
methods were the same . . . and yet how vast a difference in those three crosses.

There was the cross of rebellion.

There was the cross of repentance.

There was the cross of redemption.

Let us look at each of them in turn.

I

There was, first, the cross of rebellion. I am thinking,
of course, of the thief who derided Him in the hour of
His dying. I wonder by what path that man came to
the cross?

Did he come out of a bad home—and learn to steal
almost as soon as he learned to walk?

Did he come out of a good home, and did his
mother dream dreams concerning him and pray that
he might be good and great?

Were there bad companions who led him astray?

I do not know. But I do know how wrong he was.
He was coarsened and hardened in sin. He was no
first offender. Not even the solemnities of death
could wipe the blasphemies from his lips. He could
see Jesus, and hear Him pray for His murderers' pardon, and look upon the weeping women, and catch
the moan of His broken-hearted mother—and still spit
out his foul aspersions.

'Art not Thou the Christ?' he says, in a raucous

and derisive voice. 'Save Thyself and us.' He was bitter, spurning the good even on the day of his dying, and cursing his way to Hell in the most solemn hour of all history.

His was a cross of rebellion. His own comrade said of their condemnation that it was truly deserved, but this rebel would not learn even on the lip of the grave. He was dying with the Saviour and—wonder of wonders!—he had the chance even then to change his cross to a crown. But he threw it away.

There are people like that today. They have a cross, and the cross makes them more bitter than they were. It might be a punishment—as with the rebellious thief —or it might be an affliction which they could not help, or it might be a wrong cruelly done them by another. But instead of wresting it to their good, they twist it to their greater loss.

Here is a woman who lost her husband in early life. I know this woman. She has gone in bitterness all her widowed days. She hates God and man. She broods over her sorrow and has become a jaundiced recluse. I tremble sometimes for her reason. O yes! it was a great sorrow. Let no one speak as though the path of the widow is an easy one, or that it is simple to lose your mate in early life and go on in brave loneliness. I do not forget the courage it calls for, but I deplore the venom that fills her heart. Hers is a cross of rebellion.

Here is another woman. Years and years ago she lost her only child—a little girl of six. I never saw the child, though I have seen her photograph time and time again. This woman also is in arms against Heaven. She has never accepted her sorrow in her heart. She accuses God. I have seen her snatch open the cupboard in which the little girl kept her toys, and seen the toys spill out all over the kitchen floor. Waving her hand over them, this inconsolable mother would weep afresh. So this mother lives—if living it can be called—with an open wound which God could close in a night. The scar would still be there—but not the wound. She will not have it so! Her cross is a cross of rebellion!

And here is a man I know (in thirty years of ministry one gets to know a lot of people) who has lost his health and blames God for it. Those who knew him in his youth tell me that he had something to do with the loss of his health himself. 'George was a gay bird,' they say. 'George went the pace, you know. . . .' I do not know the truth about that. I only know this, that there is no admission in his heart that his loss of fitness might be a punishment for past indulgence, the inexorable outworking of the laws of health, the solemn justice of the universe which says that certain consequences follow on certain sins as night follows day. I only know that his cross is a cross of rebellion.

Is there anyone reading this now, crucified on a cross of rebellion; twisting the cross, as it were, and doubling its pain by missing its ministry?

Maybe you are just resigned. I can be glad for that, but you do know (don't you?) that resignation is not a

Christian grace? Always, beneath resignation, there is a pus-point of rebellion surviving still. The fully Christian are not resigned to the will of God, or acquiescent in it, or just conformed by it, but *abandoned* to it.

Are you abandoned to the will of God?

We used to sing:

> *My God, my Father, while I stray*
> *Far from my home in life's rough way,*
> *O teach me from my heart to say,*
> > *Thy will be done.*

> *If Thou should'st call me to resign*
> *What most I prize it ne'er was mine;*
> *I only yield Thee what was Thine:*
> > *Thy will be done.*

That hymn is omitted from many hymn-books now. It was left out by the true discernment of those who held that resignation is only half a Christian virtue, because there lurks beneath it something of rebellion still. There must be no rebellion. Not merely what God does, but what God allows, must win our willing acceptance. After all, it is His world, and He allows nothing out of which He cannot bring good.

II

The cross of repentance.

I am thinking now, of course, of the penitent thief. I wonder how he came to the cross. Had he a good home? Who put into him in his tenderest years that sense of decency which was still a sediment in his soul when he was suddenly selected for a minor role on the day when our Lord died at Calvary? I will love this bad man for ever. The last kind word spoken to my dying Lord was spoken by the penitent thief. He could have had only the vaguest idea what was happening—but years and years in sin had not so blunted his moral perceptions that he was incapable of recognizing a good man.

Jesus was no good man. It moved in the half-fuddled brain of this felon as he hung on the cross that he had witnessed something not of this earth. He had seen them nail the Nazarene to the wood, watched the blood spurt, forethought his own immediate agony in the writhing body of Jesus, and heard through the hammer-strokes—not the torrent of curses that was customary—but a prayer that shivered to the sky and struck into the soul of that convicted thief as nothing else had done in years: 'Father . . . forgive them . . . they know not what they do.'

He believed it then—all he had heard of Jesus. He had done nothing amiss. However fairly he himself was condemned, it was a filthy parody of justice to nail this unearthly prisoner to the cross. As the shadows gathered about him, and he heard the blasphemous railings of his companion in crime, he rebuked him. Evil man though he was, he feared God.

No man is wholly evil in whose soul still lingers some fear of God. And as he spoke, faith rose in his soul; fear, and hope, and strange remembered tales of Jesus mingled in his mind, and rushed in appeal from his parched lips. 'Jesus,' he cried, 'Jesus . . . remember me when Thou comest in Thy kingdom.'

And Jesus said: 'Verily I say unto thee, Today shalt thou be with Me in Paradise.'

Oh! the joy—in the pain—for Jesus.

He had said: 'And I, if I be lifted up from the earth, will draw all men unto Me.'

And He was lifted up—and they were coming. Already! The first of many millions. Coming, coming, yes they are.

> *The dying thief rejoiced to see*
> *That fountain in his day;*
> *And there may I . . .*

And there may you!

You.

Repentance—by a cross!

There are things to be learned in suffering and frustration which (it seems) many folk can learn no other way. I believe that God would often teach us in other ways if we would have it so, but our stubborn, obdurate hearts resist.

He tells us that war is awful, and an abrogation of His holy will, but the mass of people, with their minds bent upon pleasure, treat the warning lightly and seem unwilling to believe until blasted cities and mangled bodies force the fearful truth into their stubborn minds.

Yet the suffering is not sterile if repentance is born : repentance by a cross.

Karl Barth says : 'God enters through a breach.'

You see what he means?

When things are well with us we are not aware of our need of God. It is, so often, the consciousness of defeat, of sin, of frustration, that makes us aware of our need of Him. When our self-assurance is fatally wounded, when we quite honestly don't know what to do, when we drink to the dregs the cup of defeat, when our defences are down and our pride humbled —God enters through the breach.

Sooner or later, those who live come to some kind of Calvary in their life. It may seem to happen by chance, or by the cruelty or neglect of others, or by our own folly, ignorance, sin or mistake, but the big question still remains : 'What shall I make of my Calvary? What can I do with my cross?'

Do what the dying thief did. If anything of personal guilt mingles in it at all, make it a cross of repentance.

III

The third cross—the central cross—was the cross of redemption, and to the foot of that cross are we now come. To no holier spot than this can we ever hope to come on earth. It is, indeed, the

> *trysting place where Heaven's love*
> *And Heaven's justice meet.*

No true comparisons are . possible. This is the unique cross. Only the cross of Christ is the cross of redemption, and even to use the term of the trials which beset us is almost to prostitute the holy word. Had Christ not Himself encouraged us to use it, no reverent soul would ever speak of his own 'cross'. Yet He said: 'Whosoever doth not bear his cross and come after Me, cannot be My disciple.'

Nevertheless, only the cross of Jesus can redeem. We human beings may know in our folly the cross of rebellion, and we may know in our wisdom the cross of repentance, but in the deepest sense of the word, only Jesus knows the cross of redemption. Moreover, something was done on Calvary which needed never to be done again. In some mysterious way, it is finished work. It cannot be added to, and it cannot be taken from.

Yet—having said that—is it not true that Paul confessed to the Philippians that he longed to know the fellowship of our Lord's sufferings, and even spoke to the Colossians of 'filling up' what was 'lacking of the afflictions of Christ'? Imagine! Filling up what was lacking of the afflictions of Christ!

All that he meant by that deep word is beyond our present concern, and is, indeed, so deep a subject that 'all our thoughts are drowned'. Yet it does embolden us to say that God, in His infinite mercy, makes redemptive use of the crosses we mortals bear. It is true that

Every cross grows light beneath
The shadow, Lord, of Thine,

but it is true, also, that He can take our crosses and
turn them to redemptive use. Our bitter woes need not
run to waste. If we will allow Him, He will take the
worst experiences of our life and turn them into something healing and restorative and redeeming, not only
in our own lives, but in the lives of other people as
well.

I was in Wookey in Somerset one day and as I
passed through the wee village, I thought not only on
its famous hole but on its famous son. Born in the
home of the curate and baptized 'Cyril Arthur' by his
father, he came, after schooling, to London, and was
soon a power in Fleet Street. He had a flair for jour-
nalism. Education for all had produced millions of
shallow readers. What could they read? He gave them
—naming it after himself!—*Pearson's Weekly, Home
Notes, Pearson's Magazine*, the *Daily Express.*—The
little lad from Wookey had arrived.

And then (it was 1913), in the midst of an amazing
career, he went blind. The process had been going on
for years, but the last bit of hope vanished in 1913.

Blind!

Would you call that a cross? To live for books—and
go blind?

What did he do?

He had his doubly dark hours, I have no doubt,
but he did not rebel, or curse God, or turn sour. Did

he remember the training of his early days? his boy-
hood prayers? his father's teaching? I do not know. I
know this. He offered to God his weakness and dis-
ability, and asked the Almighty—as Milton did—if
He had use for a blind man. And God whispered in
his ear.

He obeyed! Henceforth—knowing now as never
before what it meant to be blind—he dedicated all
that remained of life to those who walked in darkness,
and expected so to walk till they died. He became—
noble contradiction of the New Testament word—the
Blind Leader of the Blind.

Soon he founded St Dunstan's; welcomed home
despairing boys as they streamed back blinded in the
first World War; taught them to hope again, to laugh,
to work, to be wanted; taught them because he knew
it all himself; gave them the tonic of a purpose in life,
and saved the reeling reason of thousands.

Well?—what do you say? Did God make redemptive use of Cyril Pearson's cross?

I hold that He did.

He could do the same with your trouble. Of all the
wicked waste that goes on in this world, no waste is
more wicked than wasted pain.

And it need not be! Foolish as it may seem to some
of you who suffer, I assert my belief that God can turn
any suffering to redemptive use. Yours; mine.

Look at them again—those three crosses on the
Hill.

The cross of rebellion.

The cross of repentance.

The cross of redemption.

Which cross is yours? Not the cross of rebellion, I trust. A cross of repentance I hope—and (in the shadow of His cross) a cross of redemption as well.

CHAPTER SEVEN

THE PEOPLE WHO MINISTERED TO HIM

A FRIEND of mine—a minister in the north of England —had a son in the Royal Air Force who was captured by the Japanese in the Second World War. In all the long years of their son's captivity, my friend and his wife only heard two or three times, but their conviction that the lad would come home safely never wavered, and indeed was greatly nourished by the fact that one of his few letters arrived only a month or two before the end of the war. His mother kept his bed aired and his room ready.

'Any day,' she said, when the prisoners began to arrive, 'my boy will come home.'

And then one day, there came a knock at the door and a soldier stood there. He was a stranger to them.

'Does Dr —— live here?' he said. 'I was with your boy when he died. I came to give you news of his end.'

The soldier did not know that this was the first intimation they had received. No doubt he would have been less direct had he known. The poor mother staggered into the house with a great cry, and my friend asked the soldier in to hear the tale of his boy's brave end.

And do you know what has consoled that broken-hearted mother since? First, of course, her belief that her boy is safe in Heaven and that she will see him again; secondly, that he is out of the pain, and weariness, and suffering he had long endured.

And then this: she dwells on all who were kind to her boy during his agony. From one and another she has gathered a good deal of information. One rough soldier risked his life every day for three months to steal a little extra nourishment from the cookhouse for her lad. To take food like that was punishable by death, but he took it daily to help his dying friend.

Another lad used to read to him when he was beyond reading himself, and several of them made a practice of talking to him daily to keep alive in him the hope of home. He was brave and inwardly composed when he died. He had fought a good fight; he had kept the faith. His mind oscillated between his two homes at the last: England, Heaven; Heaven, England. And he was truly grateful for the kindness of his friends.

Those kindnesses did not end with the dying boy. They lived in the heart of his mother: she spoke of them constantly, as well she might. 'Wasn't it brave of that dear boy to risk his life for my lad? Wasn't it kind of them to read my letters to him over and over again?' She dwelt on the mitigations of the agony of one she loved.

And that is what I want to do now. I have been reading again all the accounts of my Lord's agony with one thought in mind: who was kind to Him then? Who helped—if only a little—when all the world turned against Him? Who *wanted* to help even if they could not, but blessed Him by their sympathy? I have put it all together—familiar, known to you of old, but so comforting after studying the crueller aspects of the Passion. When the weight of the world's wickedness on the back of the world's Redeemer is almost too much for a sensitive soul to stand, there is comfort in remembering the people who were kind.

I

Let me rapidly remind you of those who ministered to our Lord in the last hours of His earthly life.

1. There was the man who carried the Cross for Him: Simon of Cyrene.

I know he was *compelled* to do it. A prisoner was supposed to carry his own cross to the place of execution, but our blessed Lord could not do it. Weakened by the bloody sweat, and the lashing of the pillar, and all the burden of the world's pain thrust through the channels of His mighty heart, He fell beneath the load.

The soldiers caught hold of a man in the crowd and made him carry the Cross. I don't suppose he wanted to. I imagine he felt as you would feel, if you were looking on at some trouble in the streets and were suddenly pounced upon to take part in it. Your first thought would be: 'I want to keep out of this.' But when he was dragged forward and saw that piteous, blood-stained figure, and the unearthly look of the Son of God, don't you think some pity stirred in his heart? Don't you think he said within himself, 'Well, I am not going to be crucified, but I can at least carry the Cross for Him'? Anyhow, he did. He carried the Cross for Jesus. I am grateful to Simon of Cyrene for that.

2. There was the soldier who moistened His lips when He cried: 'I thirst.'

Have you ever really thirsted? I wonder. The only time I ever thirsted was when I was travelling across the desert; the car broke down, and we were far from water of any kind. I would say quite positively that thirst is far more terrible than hunger.

Think of the day of the Crucifixion: the heat, and the noise, and the dust, and the pain—and the thirst. The only cry of physical torment wrung from the lips of our dying Lord was this: 'I thirst.'

Seven times He spoke—but only once of His own sufferings: 'I thirst.' And then that rough soldier darted forward and moistened his lips. Say what you like about it, it was kind—a spot of pity in the midst of hate. Never forget that there is often a kind heart beneath a rough exterior.

I soldiered once with a blaspheming Irishman who was my pet aversion, but one day, as we marched, we fell in with what today would be called a horde of 'displaced persons', and there was a little child among them utterly lost. And then that blaspheming Irishman tossed his rifle to a comrade, picked up the little girl, and carried her on his shoulder for miles and miles and miles. I always looked on him differently after that.

And there was a rough soldier who moistened my Saviour's lips.

3. There were those people who provided the drugged wine. You remember that?

It seems that there was in Jerusalem a kind of guild of benevolent women who, in order to help the many people who were crucified in those days (because, of course, crucifixion was common enough then), used to provide drink which was partly drugged so that those poor souls might have the edge taken off their agony. That drink was offered to Jesus.

He refused it. He meant to go to His Father with unclouded mind, but I have no doubt at all that He judged the deed by its intention, and the purpose behind it would have warmed His heart. It was meant well. It was another illustration—a little illustration— of pity in what must have seemed a pitiless world.

Never think that there has been no value in something you have done of good intent even if it failed in its immediate object.

Years ago I heard of someone in trouble—in need of money, as I thought. So I got the money together and made the journey to them, and I delicately led the conversation to the purpose of my coming. But when I produced the money, they were quite firm. They would not accept it. Perhaps I looked a little bit crest-fallen after that, for they hastened to assure me that I would never know what the kindness meant to them— the thought, and the effort, and the journey, and the purpose. They would not take the money; but, they said, nothing would ever take from them the memory of what I meant to do.

So, I think, it must have been with Jesus. He de-clined the drugged wine—but He blessed the purpose of those who proffered it. I am grateful to the people who offered Him the wine.

4. There was the little company of His own dear ones and friends who stood near the Cross. There was His mother and, there was John, and—farther off— Mary Magdalene, and Mary the mother of James the Less, and other holy women.

Oh, I know they didn't *do* anything—but what can you do when a dear one is dying?

I have been at hundreds of deathbeds (and at many when the one who was passing away was fully aware of what was happening and knew there was nothing more to be done)—and what do you suppose was the commonest request of people in those circumstances? Just this. They would say to their dearest: 'Stay with me ... stay with me.' They knew their dear ones could not do anything but they wanted them to stay with them.

Now that is human—and our Lord was human as well as divine. I am certain it comforted Him to know that in the midst of all that howling, fiendish rabble, there were those loving Him all the time and meaning to stay there till the end.

Crucifixion was a very shameful thing. To be transfixed, stark naked, in the gaze of a multitude of men and women must, in all conscience, be an experience beyond our power to imagine, and it was as though His dear ones were saying: 'Whatever shame there is in this . . . so far as we can bear it . . . we are sharing it with you.'

I am grateful to His dear ones that they stood by and shared the shame and sustained Him with their sympathy.

5. Lastly—but in some ways, chiefly—I am grateful to the penitent thief of whom I have already written. Isn't it an amazing thing that the last kind word spoken to Jesus was spoken by a thief?

Even in His agony our Lord must have exulted in the potency of His Cross. It is the Cross that pierces hard hearts. Have not millions truly said:

At the Cross! At the Cross! Where I first saw the light
And the burden of my heart rolled away?

I shall love the penitent thief for ever because he spoke that last kind word to Jesus Christ.

Well, there are they—the people who were kind to Jesus in His passion, and for the memory of whom I bless my God whenever I linger at the Cross. Not everybody who came to Calvary came to scoff. Some came of love, and may have put themselves in peril by coming. It is their undying distinction that they ministered to their dying Lord.

II

'But what practical relevance,' you might ask, 'has this to our life today? What does it matter *now*?'

That is not hard to answer.

The author of the Epistle to the Hebrews says that there are spiritual senses in which it is possible to crucify the Son of God afresh. Indeed, there are senses in which sin is doing that all the time. What a pain it must be in the heart of Jesus to see this world, for which He died nigh two thousand years ago, so indifferent to His Gospel, and countries, nominally Christian, staining the name they so unworthily bear.

Let me give you one simple illustration of what I mean.

For many, many years, Christian missionaries, most of them from Australia, were busy in New Guinea. New Guinea had had very little contact with the outer world except through missionaries, but the work had been so successful that long before the last war broke out the Christian Church had built in New Guinea a company of faithful Christian people who repeated, in many ways, the simplicity and purity of the early Church. When the war came, some of the missionaries were killed and some were driven away, and there was little dependable information for years about the Church in New Guinea.

Then the missionaries got back again. What a terrible tale they had to tell! They said that they found 'a wounded Church'. Many of the members of the Church were literally wounded—maimed, and halt, and blind—because of the fighting. But that was not the most serious thing. Some of the greatest damage done to the Church had been done by the white soldiers who were there, many of whom had made utter mockery of the simple faith of those coloured people, and some of whom had been guilty of the foulest assaults upon the women of those primitive parts.

Those simple people had supposed that folk who came from Christian lands were Christian people, and their horror when they discovered that they had to protect their women from the licentiousness of those who, being white outside, they supposed to be white inside, knew no bounds. Some of the missionaries who got back to them almost wished that they had died themselves. 'Pray for us,' they said, 'as we face the terrible task of rebuilding the Church in New Guinea.'

What must all this have meant to our Lord? Think of the wickedness which has gone on in this world: the concentration camps, the butchery, the lies, the immorality. What a pain in the heart of the Saviour! There are senses in which our Lord's Crucifixion is drawn out through all the years. He wants to 'present us faultless before His Father's face', but how tragically we impede His work.

Yet, if it be true that His passion persists still, it must be true also that it is possible still to minister to

Him in His passion. I reason that, if it is possible to crucify Him afresh, it must be possible to serve Him afresh; that I, and you, can carry the Cross for Jesus, like Simon of Cyrene; that we can moisten His parched lips, like that rough but pitying soldier; that we can share the shame of Calvary, like His mother and John; that we can prove to Him the power of His Cross, like the dying thief.

All this we can do.

Are you doing it? Let me press that question upon you. Are you doing it? Carrying the Cross? Moistening His lips? Sharing the shame? Proving to Him the power of His Cross?

III

1. Wherever men and women engage in Christlike service, there they are bearing the Cross for Jesus.

Did you ever hear of Dr Brackett? Perhaps not. He ministered, as a medical practitioner, in a small town in the southern parts of the United States. But I think you ought to know about Dr Brackett. He specialized in serving poor people who had no money. He would get up on the coldest night and go for miles to help some needy soul. Everybody knew his surgery. It was on the main street over a clothing store, and there was a plate at the doorway. He never married. He fell in love, but on the day of his wedding he was called out to the birth of a Mexican child, and his girl gave him up. She said that a man who would fail to appear at his wedding for the sake of a Mexican child would not any good as her husband. A lot of people agreed with her, but not, I need hardly say, the parents of that little Mexican child.

He died when he was over seventy. It was the biggest funeral they had ever had in that town or neighbourhood. And then they began to argue about a fitting memorial—what should be inscribed upon it, and how tall it should be.

But, as often happens, it all ended in talk, and the only people who seemed really worried were the parents of the child he had delivered all those years before, on the day which should have been his wedding day. They settled the memorial in the end. It was the undertaker who discovered what they had done. Too poor themselves to put up a stone, they went at night and took from the door of his old office the brass plate that had been there so many years. Passing through the cemetery, the undertaker noticed it. Embedded in a mass of flowers, he read the old inscription:

Dr Brackett
Office Upstairs

I say again: wherever men and women engage in Christlike service, caring for the sick and needy, and doing it for love, there they are bearing the Cross of Jesus.

2. I go farther. I say that whenever anyone stands by his needy brothers and seeks to share their blame, there he moistens the lips of Jesus, and there he helps

Him in His agony.

It is no longer disputed today that, by scientific standards of nutrition, over one half of the world is hungry and a third of it is starving. Moreover, the world grows smaller. The swift liner, and the swifter jet, have made the earth a neighbourhood. Broadcasting and television spread a nation's news over all the globe in moments, and the cinema has penetrated to the jungle to portray the comparative opulence of Western life to the starving multitudes of the East.

The uncounted Millions of China and India want their place also at the feast. They are industrious, thrifty and very fertile, and their half-empty stomachs lie behind the political and ideological ferment of the world. When people are hungry, and so miserable that no situation could be worse, they are ready for revolution. 'Nothing', they say, 'could be worse than this.' Even the offer of 'freedom' seems academic to them when the body is crying out for rice.

Meanwhile, people in the Western World live on in the illusion that national frontiers are still important, and that the maintenance of their high standard of living is a sacred duty. Cars, radio sets, refrigerators, and television seem more important to them than that their fellow-men should have one meal a day. If they can be persuaded to consider the problem at all, they make some airy reference to the necessity to 'level-up' rather than to 'level-down', and picture a world in which everybody will have cars, radio sets, refrigerators, and television. How that can possibly be in the world as we know it, they do not pause to explain. How a white élite can live on the toil of the black and brown and yellow men, as though white men have a divine right to a higher standard of living, is never made clear. Even responsible statesmen promise that the British standard of living can be twice as high in twenty-five years, though many major signs tell against it, and an awful economic blizzard could blow upon the whole structure and reduce it in a couple of years to a terrible austerity.

Yet Christ died for all. His 'undistinguishing regard' moves out to all the children of men. In Him no racial superiorities and inferiorities can have any place. The prize He offers to the privileged is to share their privileges with those who are without them.

Nor does He lack far-sighted servants who are seeking to work out His purposes in the most sacrificial ways, who are seeking the Christian answer to economic problems, who want to know how goods can be *given* without creating industrial chaos, who can prove the practical outworkings of Christian love, who know within themselves that to work for the glory of God is a greater incentive than to work for material gain, who can see the Divine relation of the material and the spiritual and demonstrate it in their own devoted lives.

Whoever so lives is moistening the lips of the Saviour, whether it be an Albert Schweitzer living as a missionary-doctor in the steaming heat of the Gabon, or a Toyohiko Kagawa in the slums of Tokyo, or a Frank Laubach fighting illiteracy, or a George Carver solving agricultural problems by prayer at a laboratory bench.

There are thousands of others like them, unknown to fame and self-severed from fortune. Christ knows them. They give Him a drink on the Cross.

3. I go farther still. Wherever any brave soul faces the God-denying look of things, and still trusts God even in the shadows, there the example of Jesus, who trusted His Father even when He seemed deserted on the Cross, is gloriously emulated.

I wrote just now about the sad situation of the Church in New Guinea. I had a letter from the relatives of some of my friends who are missionaries there.

I knew that they had had a terrible time. Their house had been burned to the ground, and all their possessions stolen. Nine years of hard work in translating the Scriptures, and in shaping a dictionary, had all been wasted; the Bible Society were waiting to print but the papers had perished. The missionary himself was afflicted with a terrible skin disease, and had some trouble with his kidneys, due to long exposure in the sodden climate. His wife was ill also. And I had written to ask: 'What is the state of mind of these people who have suffered so much and seem deserted by their God, who have seen the things to which they gave themselves broken, their own health gone, the future all unknown? Tell me, what is their testimony now?'

The letter I received from their relatives was the reply. It just said: 'Their faith is unshaken. They assert that God is good.' Just that. Just like the Saviour hanging transfixed upon the Cross and saying: 'God is love'; illustrating it by His dying; showing us, in a moment of time, what God is through all eternity.

God be praised that there are these ministries open to us still: that we can carry the Cross for Jesus; moisten His lips; share His shame; prove, by our own devotion, the potency of His dying.

CHAPTER EIGHT

I WAS THERE, TOO

WE have looked at the many roads by which the people implicated in the death of Christ travelled to Calvary. Another task awaits us now. We, also, must make this journey. Every man and woman must come, sooner or later, to the Cross. The meaning, and the power, and the preciousness of it will elude us unless we see that we were involved in it too; unless, in short, we can honestly say with St Paul: 'The Son of God, who loved *me* and gave Himself up for *me*.'

Yet that is the hard part of the Cross to multitudes of people—how to get 'me' into it, how to see that it matters to them personally, enormously, eternally. Fifty-seven generations separate us from those who stood on that first Good Friday by the green hill outside the city wall. St Paul was our Lord's contemporary, living at the same time and conversing with those who knew Him well. There may be a sense in which he could say intelligently: 'The Son of God, who loved *me* and gave Himself up for *me*'; but how can I say that—and how can you? I wasn't thought of then—not humanly, anyhow—and neither were you; the slow unfolding of many ages was to elapse before the opportunity of life should be mine or yours. How, then, can it be said with truth that 'He loved me, and gave Himself up for me'?

And yet the Crucifixion is powerless without that personal note in it. If I honestly cannot see its reference to me, if the pronouns are misconceived and irrelevant, then it is just an event of ancient history, like the fall of Babylon, or the march of the Ten Thousand, or the death of Socrates, which are of interest to the historian but cannot truly be said to matter much today and much to me. How can I get the 'me' into the Crucifixion? How can I say with sincerity that 'He loved *me*, and gave Himself up for *me*?'

Now it was just getting the 'me' into the Cross which made all the difference to the greatest figures of evangelical religion. It was that realization in the main that made them the men they were.

It was true of Paul, for he it was who first used these words.

It was true of Luther. In his early years he was a rigid Roman monk, laboriously working his passage to heaven by midnight vigils, and flagellations, and fastings, and still never feeling that his sins were forgiven, until that ever-memorable day when the pronouns came alive to him and he cried: 'The Son of God, who loved *me*, and gave Himself up for *me*.' Writing his commentary on Galatians years afterwards he said: 'Read therefore with great vehemency these words, "*me* and for *me*", and so inwardly practise with thyself, that thou, with a sure faith, mayst con-

ceive and print this "me" in thy heart, and apply it
unto thyself, not doubting but thou art of the number
of those to whom this "me" belongeth.'

It was so with John Wesley, too. Whatever it was
that happened in Aldersgate Street on 14th May 1738,
there is no question that the pronouns came alive. He
says himself : '. . . an assurance was given me that He
had taken away *my* sins, even *mine*, and saved *me*
from the law of sin and death.'

Nor was it different with Charles, his brother, who
came into the experience a day or two before John.
The 'me' came into it suddenly for him. He cried :

> *I felt my Lord's atoning blood*
> *Close to my soul applied;*
> Me, me *He loved—the Son of God,*
> *For* me, *for* me *He died.*

Or, if I may take a similar illustration from another
school of religious thought, I would remind you of St
Teresa. She had been in the convent some time before
the great experience came, but being in a convent had
not meant very much to her then—lots of Spanish
girls went into convents in her time, and do still. But
she was entering her oratory one day and saw a picture
of Christ being scourged, and for the first time, the
'me' of it came over her with overwhelming power.
To herself she said : 'He did it all for me.' And, as a
result of that, she had, all the days of her life, what she
called 'a sense of unpayable debt'. If you want to

understand the labours and sufferings of St Teresa, you will have to trace it to the day when the 'me' came into the Cross and gave her that sense of unpayable debt.

Certainly, then, if we are to enter into the wonder and living power of the Cross we must get the 'me' into it. Let me try, therefore, to answer the difficulties which people have expressed to me at different times about this personal reference of the Cross.

I

How could He die for my sins if over nineteen hundred years were to pass before I committed any?
This is my answer: He not only died *for* your sins; He died *by* your sins.

You know what I mean by that. Earlier in this book I have stressed this solemn and neglected fact: that Jesus Christ was not done to death by a few peculiarly wicked sins committed by a few monsters of iniquity. He was done to death by an accumulation of ordinary sins, the same sins that you and I have committed, and that some of us, maybe, are committing still.

There was the bigotry of the Pharisees—and we have been bigoted; there was the self-seeking of the Sadducees—and we have been self-seeking; there was the anxiety of Pilate, when he thought his own position was in peril, to secure himself at the sacrifice of someone else—and we have been guilty of that; there was the cheap taunt of the unreflecting crowd—and all of us have joined in angry clamour at some time or other against men who did not deserve it, men whom we did not know, and could have given no better reason for our censorious judgement than that other people were saying it too.

Those were the sins that nailed Jesus Christ on the wood, and we have committed those very sins. Who can stand up and say he has never been selfish, never been bigoted, never had his eye to the main chance, never been guilty of tainted gossip? Not one of us.

Of course, we never understood what those sins could do until we saw the Cross. It never broke on our mind that that kind of thing could lead to this kind of consequence. But it could—and it did.

Maybe you feel, even as you read this, that you are a good fellow and have never done anyone a bad turn. But that is only because the consequences of ordinary sins have never come home to you. Does it come home now? Do you see that that is one of the purposes of the Cross—to make us see plainly what is normally hid, the foulness and deadly nature of common sins. Next time you see a crucifix at some wayside memorial, or on the wall of a church, pause—and think—and say: I did that.'

II

How could a thing be done for me so many genera-
tions before I was born?
Because a thing was done before you were born, it is not done any less for you, if, in point of fact, you benefit by it in the hour of your great need.

I mean this.

Have you ever had an operation—a major operation? Do you remember the chill stab at the heart when the doctor said, 'It must be an operation'? Did you ever feel, before that solemn half-hour when the doctor broke it to you, how important anaesthetics were? It is not so very long ago that there were no anaesthetics.

I had to read, not long ago, of the work of the surgeons on board His Majesty's Ship *Victory* at the Battle of Trafalgar. It was almost too much to read. I could not even hint at it to you—the awful amputations and carving about of human flesh, without anaesthetics. Just picture, for a moment, what a major operation would have been ... *without anaesthetics*.

But when the doctor told you that you had to be operated upon, you had not that awful thing to face. You could, at least, begin to comfort yourself at once by saying: 'Well, I shan't *feel* it.' How grateful you must have been then for anaesthetics.

Of course, they were discovered before you were born—but they were discovered *for* you, weren't they? You felt it in that moment, didn't you? When the doctor said, 'I am afraid it must be an operation', you saw then that, although it was discovered before you were born, it was for you, for that very hour when your need was discovered, for *you*.

You did not argue with yourself in that moment that it was not discovered for you alone? You did not say that Sir James Young Simpson, when at last he found chloroform, was not thinking of you as an individual. You did not reason in that shallow way. In that hour of your great need, as you remembered your great help, you felt in your heart: It was for me; for *me*.

No serious theologian has ever taught that when our Lord hung upon the Cross and died for us, He thought individually of the teeming millions who would claim an interest in His blood—but still it was for you. It avails for you. You can say with truth:

> *This all my hope and all my plea,*
> *For me the Saviour died.*

III

What is the essential difference between the death of Christ and the death of a martyr?

It turns on who the person was.

People who think of Christ as a superior martyr (and many, even in the Churches, have slipped half-unconsciously into this false way of thinking) are thinking of Christ only as a good man. He is not incarnate God; or at least, his divine nature, in their thinking, has been so swallowed up by His humanity that in any sovereign saving way He has ceased to be God at all. He is a pathetic figure whom wicked men can handle how they will.

It is not hard to understand how even pious people, undisciplined in thinking, can come to take that erroneous view. To put the stress entirely on the human activity in this cosmic event and to see Christ only as a passive victim, meekly enduring whatever man will inflict upon Him, is to see but half the truth—the lesser half. Though the guilt of the death of Christ was shared by the teachers who hated Him and the priests who bought Him, the traitor who sold Him and the judge who sentenced Him, *He* had a will in it all the time—the chief will; the ruling, determining, effective will.

He *consented* to it. Indeed, there are senses in which He sought it. He laid Himself on the wood. What they freely sought, He freely sought as well. He could have stepped from the Cross as easily as I could fling down this pen and tear up this page. His death was the end of their foul deed, schemed for, cunningly contrived, and fiendishly achieved. His death was the crown of His sublime deed, planned in heaven, wrought out on earth, and gloriously consummated on those two pieces of wood.

Those devils and weaklings who met at Calvary would have said: 'We did it.' He cries from His Cross: 'I did it! It is finished!' If they were right, the Cross would be a gibbet, a symbol of shame, something to hide and speak of only by compulsion and with bated breath. In point of fact, we placard it to all the world. No steeple so high that it will not bear it; no point of earth but is honoured to be the stump of His Cross; it even lies in a cache on the summit of Everest left by the first British expedition. It is His message, not theirs, which it bears at the last.

That free and evil men sought and secured His death cannot alter the fact that He knew what they were doing—and let them do it. You cannot martyr *God*. God could not have His life *taken* from Him. Hold in mind all the time *who* it was who hung and suffered there, and you will not think of it as martyrdom.

If He was a man, it was murder; if He was God, it was an offering.

If He was a man, it was martyrdom; if He was God, it was sacrifice.

If He was man, they took His life from Him; if He was God, He laid it down of Himself.

If He was man, we are called to admiration; if He was God, we are called to adoration.

If He was man, we must stand up and take our hats off; if He was God, we must fall down and give Him our hearts.

If you come to Calvary with some admiration of His life and some pity at His death, and see in Him nothing but another good man beaten by the wickedness of the world, you have not really come to Calvary at all. No mere man could save you. The teaching of the Church Universal is this: the immortal God has died for you.

IV

Why do I need a Saviour at all?
Why do you need a Saviour at all?
Go back to the Cross!

When we were looking just now at the Cross and considering the sins that put Jesus there, you recognized, I think, that they were *your* sins, and recognized it in a way you had not, perhaps, recognized before. The Cross revealed it to you. That is one of the wonderful things about the Cross. It begins by revealing our sins.

That is the kind of person you are. Don't shrink from it. Don't say you are not. Don't announce again: 'I have never done anyone a bad turn.' I don't believe it. I *do* believe that you have not realized how bad a turn you have been doing people. But by your selfishness (which is inbred in you and in me), by your bigotry, by your light and shallow talk, by many other things you know and God knows, you are really shot through with sin; you are dyed in it, and dyed in the wool.

The Cross has opened your eyes to it. It has shown you what you are—and you can do nothing about it. You cannot, of yourself, wash out the past, and you cannot, with confidence, expect to overcome in the future. That is where you are, and I say reverently, 'God help you', because nobody else can.

What are you going to do about it? What are you going to do about the past which you cannot undo, and the future in which, without supernatural help, you will commit the same sins again and again?

Do you think you can make up your little mind never to be selfish again, and keep that resolution all on your own? You cannot do it. That is why I advise:

'Go to the Cross'. There is nowhere else for helpless sinners to go. Go to the Cross. Plead, as earnestly as a skilful advocate before a judge. But don't defend yourself. The case is lost if you do that. Don't base your plea on justice. Plead for mercy. Ask God, for Christ's sake, to forgive you your sins.

V

Why was the Cross necessary? Why could not God forgive without it?

There are many people today—and some in the Church—who feel that the Cross was quite unnecessary. They do not pause to explain why Christ should endure as God something which was quite unnecessary. Perhaps they have half accepted the idea that His humanity required Him to endure whatever men would sink to, and that He had so emptied Himself of divine power that He could do no other than bear such evil as came.

Some of them support their view by quoting Christ's own teaching. They take the Parable of the Prodigal Son, for instance, as a complete picture of God's relationship with His wayward children, and they point out that when the prodigal was penitent and came home, his father ran out and forgave him. There was no talk of atonement, they say; the elder brother did not have to bear some punishment before the prodigal could be forgiven. The father met penitence with pardon, and that is a picture of God's dealings with sinners since the commerce of earth and heaven began: and to put the truth of their contentions beyond all doubt, they say that that is how they would deal with any wayward son of their own. If he was sorry and said so, that would be the end of it; they would forgive him at once, without reservation and without atonement either. They slyly hint that we must either abandon all thought of atonement, or tacitly admit that mortals are more magnanimous than God.

But the Parable of the Prodigal Son is not a complete picture of God's relationships with His wayward children. It was not meant to be. The relationship of a human father and his son, being the relationship of two sinners, is not, and never can be, a perfect and complete parallel of the relationship of a sinner and the Holy God.

Sin is an offence to God, an insult to His holiness so awful and affronting that no mortal can conceive how great the insult is. Only holiness can perceive holiness. The saints, who come nearest the eternal throne, learn that they are infinitely remote from the burning purity of God, but even at their remote distance, they feel upon them the breath of burning and testify that our God is a consuming fire.

But we are *not* saints. How can we hope with our sin-blinded eyes even to glimpse the holiness of God? The best we can do is to judge the nature of sin by its consequences and (having no acquaintance with worlds other than this) with its consequences on this earth.

How foul they are! Even with our myopic vision we can see the wide havoc of sin. Sin has so invaded our nature that it twists our own cleverness, and every step in science becomes a step in sin. The plane, the radio, and the splintered atom (all of them so fecund with goodness!) have been twisted to Satanic use. Sin spreads like an obscene tide over all this fair earth. It has so completely tainted our nature that even when we half-recognize it and want to escape it, we cannot. We realize, for instance, that race-war would be race-suicide, and yet we move that way. Not merely as persons but as peoples, we seem hopelessly lost, and drift to the things we dread. 'The good we would, we do not: the evil would not, that we do.'

How can people who see even so much sin as that (and how small a part it is) wave it lightly aside and suppose that a holy God could wave it lightly aside also. 'Sin doesn't matter—or not much. If you are sorry, let us forget it!' But cancer is still cancer, even when you have forgotten it, and no amount of forgetting hinders it in its deadly course. We cannot, as sinners, even recognize sin by ourselves, and a sin not fully recognized is a sin of which one cannot repent. To suppose that the sin of the world could be met, exposed and defeated, on the analogy of a human father forgiving the delinquencies of his wayward son, is to misconceive the greatness of the problem and to fail completely in the quest for a cure.

'But couldn't *God* find a way to deal with sin with-

out the Cross?' People ask. 'After all, God can do anything. Surely almightiness could have devised a
method of by-passing Calvary.'

It might be sufficient to reply by saying that God
couldn't find a way, but it would be better to point out
that God cannot do *anything*. A great deal of muddled
thinking lies behind the use of that repeated phrase.
God cannot contradict His own rationality and make a
square circle, or an aged infant, or a one-sided sheet of
paper. He cannot deny His own nature and be vindic-
tive, or evil, or unkind. Nor can He ever tolerate sin.
Between the holy God and sin there can never be
compromise, or indulgence, or neutrality. Its deadly
nature does not allow even the Divine to say: 'It does
not matter.' The central evil of sin must be met and
overcome.

Sin always takes its price and someone must pay it.
Yet even the paying of the price is not enough. The
foul principle of the thing had to be broken. It had to
be met in its innermost nature and the life taken out of
it.

The consequence of sin is death—not just the
punishment of it, the *consequence* of it. Death is in it.
It carries death in its nature more certainly than does
the virus of the most horrible plague. Infected with
this foul disease, the whole human race trod the path
to spiritual death. Nor was there anything any mortal
could do about it. The most advanced saints and seers
shared the infection. They may have understood a
little more than their neighbours the dire calamity of

our lost race, but the problem was completely beyond their solution. They could not save themselves, much less their fellows. They only knew a little more of human need.

Moreover, it belongs to the nature of sin to blind as it grows; the more you have of it, the less you see of it. That is why people who disbelieve in God and ignore His Church are always the first to protest that they are not sinners. 'What is wrong with me?' they ask, and patter again about their 'good turns'. Nothing so illustrates the lost condition of a man as his intimation (overt or covert) that he has no awareness of sin.

But the pre-requisite of all repentance is a recognition of one's sin. One cannot *prepare* to repent unless one sees sin for what it is, and how can a sin-blinded man even *see* the thing for what it is? And if he cannot recognize the sin, how can he repent it? Repentance, to be adequate, must have some relation to the depth and enormity of the wrong-doing, and one would need holiness even to recognize the sin and be moved to repentance.

In my army days in the First World War, I remember a camp on the top of a hill near Boulogne. The Medical Officer's Room was on the top of another hill some distance away. Any man 'reporting sick' was required to leave the camp and present himself with full pack and in marching order to the Medical Officer on the top of the other hill. We often smiled at the grim humour or the insanity of it. Only a man fighting fit could have reported 'sick' at all. No man really ill was capable of marching up the hill with all his kit upon him.

It is a picture of one aspect of our human dilemma. Only the holy can see sin for what it is, but if one cannot see sin for what it is, how can one repent it? So our race drifted to destruction, beaten by a problem beyond all human cure.

The central and most glorious truth of the Christian Gospel is that God, in the Person of Jesus Christ, bent to man's dilemma and did for him what he could not do for Himself. It was, indeed, a problem for God alone. Horace, in his *Ars Poetica* laying down the rules for young dramatists, warned them against the too ready use of a device employed by playwrights in that period. When their characters were entangled in difficult situations, a god would be introduced to extricate the hero or elucidate the plot. The young playwrights overdid it. Horace laid it down that, in tragedy, a god should never be introduced save to untie a knot which baffled all human skill.

That describes our human situation; it was a knot which baffled all human skill. But Christ bent to our need. He was born among us, lived our life, was tempted in all points, like as we are, suffered at the hands of sinners, and offered, as Man, a perfect repentance for our race. He exposed sin, accepted God's righteous judgement which makes punishment its consequence, sacrificed Himself in willing acceptance of the price, in some mysterious way bore the entail on

our behalf. And it was *God* who did it. Love, not vin-
dictiveness, is at its heart. Sin demands punishment in
any righteous world, and God in Christ bears the
dreadful cost. It was no pathetic, beaten figure who
cried from the Cross: 'It is finished!' It was God's
own Son, Royal, and Priestly, and Sovereign. He
alone could do it. No one else could see sin for what it
was. No one else could bear the heaped-up wickedness
of our race.

Nor was this all. In His death, the Bible teaches, He
broke the *power* of sin. In a way we do not fully com-
prehend, He devitalized it; He took the life out of death
(if the paradox can be allowed) and opened the Kingdom of Heaven to all believers. Something was done
on Calvary which needs never to be done again. On
that green hill, our Lord drew sin to battle—and beat
it. He focused evil and then exposed it. He showed it
to be the hideous thing it is. He overcame it by love;
never allowed one shaft of hate to get past Him; held
it in His mighty heart.

Nor is it enough to say that by the exposure of His
loving heart He so revealed God, that men were
changed in spirit and made eager for reconciliation.
While this is true, it is impressively incomplete. In some
deep way, He *bore* our sins: He knew (as the cry of
dereliction shows) that sense of separation from God
which is at all times sin's heaviest price; and as Representative Man, carried the sins we could not even see,
and offered a perfect penitence for the Race He dearly
loved.

All talk of God lightly forgiving sin is sentimentalism. The pillars of justice would fall in any society in which light views were taken of sin. Imagine a judge in a human court hearing a sane man plead guilty to repeated rape and poisoning and the corruption of little children, and then meeting the prisoner's professions of penitence with a kind word and a free pardon: 'If you are sorry, we will say no more about it. Be careful in future. . . .'

No society would stand where such judgements were common. Justice would cry out against it. What survived of conscience in the criminal himself would cry out against it too. Therein lies the truth of Bernard Shaw's remark that 'forgiveness is a coward's refuge. We must pay our debts.' What Shaw could not see, and thousands like him, was that God does not deal lightly with sin in His readiness to forgive us. He bears it Himself. The debt was met in Jesus. What no man could do, this Man did. He fought sin and defeated it. He found a way. Yielding ourselves to Him, we also may find the way.

But the way runs by Calvary. There can be no serious talk of the Cross as unnecessary. It is pert to the point of blasphemy for any mortal to look on Christ sweating blood in Gethsemane, or dying in agony on the Cross, and to decide that it was all unnecessary. Perhaps the shortest answer to such a suggestion would be to say that if the Cross was unnecessary, it would never have been.

VI

Is it not enough to believe that the Cross saves, without knowing how? Does it avail for those who do not understand it?

It is often said that each age has its theory of the Atonement, and that the theories do not matter very much. Volumes have been written on them. They change with changing years. 'The theories are unimportant,' it is commonly said. 'It is the Cross itself which saves.'

This statement is an amalgam of truth and falsity, and we must try to separate them.

It is true that various theories of the Atonement have been held through the centuries and that some of them are quite repugnant to us now. In those ages, no doubt, the Cross saved despite the explanations men offered of it.

It is true also that the Cross avails for any poor and devout charwoman, who would be completely lost in theological discussion, but who knows how to 'hang on a crucified God'. Her inability to explain how the Cross saves makes no difference to its saving. She looks at the sublime symbol and feels within herself, 'He did it for me', and all her trust is in Him. No serious theologian would doubt the spiritual security of that trusting soul.

I am writing this deep in a Swiss valley. A cable car swings on a thin wire overhead. It carries thirty-two people and is moving over an awful abyss at a height of 5,000 feet. I doubt if one person in that car knows how it works, how thirty-two people can be conveyed in a box of metal and glass over a great ravine on one steel wire. Does the wire move, or only the car? But how can the car go steeply upwards with no rack and pinion principle involved at all? They do not know. They do not care. Soon they will land on the mountain peak and enjoy the most heavenly views. It will avail for them, though none of them understands.

Yes, but somebody understands. The genius who conceived it—he understood. The artificer who made it—he understood. The engineers who maintain it—they understand. Heaven help those poor souls in the car if somebody does not understand! Behind their trust is the genius which planned it, and the high skill which outworked it, and the faithfulness which maintains it, and if they were not there, the people in the car would either swing helplessly in air or pitch hopelessly to death.

So it is with the Cross. It can avail for those who do not understand it so long as they trust themselves to it. *But somebody must understand!* If the theologian cannot understand *fully* (and what electrical engineer fully understands electricity?), he must understand more than the simple believers on whom the burden of thought is not laid. For the teachers of the faith to abandon the quest of understanding would be fatal. A spiritual fact, like the saving Cross, would cease to be a fact if no explanation were possible. Doubt would invade the mind. Less and less mention would be made of it. It would be ignored by one generation, declared unnecessary by the next, and denied by the third. Passengers would cease to travel by the cable car. The rumour would spread abroad that the engineers had lost faith in the thing, and nobody would land on the lofty peak to enjoy those heavenly views.

A burden of understanding is laid on all who teach the faith—and all who would hold it with firmness. Few things are more nourishing to our Christian religion than a grasp of its principles, and no greater service can be rendered to those who have a battle with honest doubt than to remove the impediments to belief. To say that full explanations elude us is humble and honest, but to say that they do not matter in intellectual suicide, and will ultimately prove fatal to the faith.

VII

Is there a special sense in which I am saved by the blood *of Christ?*

Some people insist that we are saved just by the *blood* of Christ, and sometimes they add 'literally'. It is difficult fully to understand their meaning—even after conversation with them. They test the value of every sermon and every religious book by the number of times 'the blood of Christ' appears in it, and however impregnated either may be with the Spirit of our Lord, it is waved aside as useless if it is not studded with this single phrase.

I suspect that these people feel (not without justifica-

tion) that all teaching of atonement has dropped out of
some pulpits, and so sure are they that the Atonement
is the heart of the Gospel, that they contend for it on
all occasions. If, indeed, that is the reason, we may
sympathize with their endeavours even while we recognize some confusion in their thought.

Being 'washed in the blood of Christ', when used to
indicate the means of our salvation, is a metaphor—the
most ancient, honoured, and moving metaphor known
among men, but still a metaphor. Crucifixion was the
form of public execution commonly employed by the
Romans in Palestine at the time of Christ's death. But
if our Lord had been done to death by hanging or
stoning, it would still have been the means of our salvation—so long as it had expressed His complete
obedience to His Father's will and His acceptance of
God's righteous judgement on sin. Not the flowing
blood, but the total surrender of His will 'even unto
death', lies at the heart of this sublime mystery. The
flowing blood gloriously symbolizes it, but it is in the
utter obedience, and not in the flowing blood as such,
that our salvation centres.

To be effective (so the writer believes), the death of
Christ had to be violent and official and certified. Only
a violent death could have exposed sin in the way sin
so sorely needed exposing. Only so could He lay down
His life of Himself—consenting to it in sacrifice,
thought with full power to refuse death, and at one
glance to summon the twelve legions of angels. Could
He have exposed sin in all its foul horror if He had

died in His bed, or by accident, or by disease?

Not only had His death to be violent; it had to be *official*. He could have died a violent death at the hand of a footpad, mistaken in the supposition that our Lord had a purse. It would have been violent death, and in its measure it would have exposed sin. But it would not have been 'official'. It would have been (men would have argued) the deed of 'a criminal type of individual', and no revelation of the real character of the human race.

But our Lord's death was official. The best people of His nation sought it. God's High Priest applied for it; he solemnly asserted : 'It is expedient . . . that one man should die for the people.' The people themselves said : 'His blood be on us, and on our children.' Through their highly-placed representatives, and in the mouth of misguided democracy, they *demanded* His death. When they were given a final chance to change their mind and select a prisoner for release, they screamed : 'Not this man but Barabbas !' So the Representative Man was officially offered for the slaughter. It was the deed of the nation, in as solemn and official a manner as any deed of the nation could be done.

Not only had His death to be violent and official. It had to be *certified*. The crucifixion and resurrection are all a piece. The Conqueror of Death was to come back from the grave, and it had to be *known* that He had come back from the grave. But who would believe that a man had come back from the grave? The easiest retort to any such assertion, if it were made, was that the man could *not* have been dead—even if he had appeared so.

So His death had to be certified. It was, in fact doubly certified by Jew and Roman. 'Make sure they are dead,' said the Jews, 'and clear the crosses. It is our great feast.'

'They are dead,' said the Romans, 'the Middle One died first. . . .' So He had a certified death, and therefore, an undeniable resurrection.

Violent, official, and certified were the features of His dying, but at the heart of it, and central to it, was His complete obedience. His life was taken from Him? Yes. But that is not the saving truth. The deeper, diviner truth is this : He laid it down of Himself.

It is clear that a death by stoning *could* have been violent, official, and certified. The certification would have been less complete, because the Romans did not execute that way; but it *could* have been. And, with the sublime obedience at its heart, it could have been just as saving.

What is it, then, that makes the metaphor of the blood so precious and moves us even to tears?

> *His dying crimson like a robe*
> *Spreads o'er His Body on the tree;*
> *Then I am dead to all the globe,*
> *And all the globe is dead to me.*

There is a deep conviction in us that the blood is the life. The Bible says so and some sense of the truth of it is in the mind of natural man as well. No man has moved through the bloody horror of battle-fields or air-raids, and seen people bleeding to death, without feeling as he watched in helplessness that the life pulsed out with the blood.

Moreover, it was among the Hebrew people that Christ was born. He could have been born only among them. They were the chosen people, and He was their Messiah. Nothing more exposes the devilry of sin than the fact that it was the descendants of the prophets, the most spiritually sensitive people on earth, who officially demanded Christ's death. When the spiritual élite of the earth fall as low as that, can anybody still believe that our race needs no Saviour and is able to save itself?

Now, the ancient ritual of the Hebrew people made much of sacrifice and the outpoured blood. Is it any wonder that the first disciples (Jews to a man) saw Jesus as the very Paschal Lamb *offering Himself*, and caught up the symbolism of the centuries as they gazed on His streaming blood?

It is no wonder.

And the devout, through nineteen centuries, have looked on those flowing wounds and caught the symbolism of it too. Crucifixion is so public. It *proclaims* death. It holds it up between earth and heaven. It placards it. And, as the blood drips from those pierced hands and feet and streams from His side, the awful pageantry of sacrifice is pressed upon us all. It is no wonder that being 'washed by the blood of Christ' has become so dear a phrase. See it as a solemn metaphor, and nothing dearer will ever come to mind. Put yourself in those pierced and bleeding hands, and know yourself for ever secure.

A friend of mine had a comrade in the last war who went into the shell-torn battle-field and brought back a wounded man. As he drew the groaning man to safety, he was fatally wounded himself. He knew before he died that the man he had rescued would live, and it was a great comfort to him as his own life ebbed away. At the last (half in delirium), he kept murmuring: 'I brought him through ... I brought him through ...'

Look at the Cross. Look at the flowing wounds.

He brought us through.

VIII

What effect can the Cross of Christ have on the whole world?

Many people complain that they cannot see the world-wide meaning of the Cross, that it does not have cosmic significance for them, that they do not understand how it can affect the life of the whole race.

The difficulty has many facets.

Some complain that they do not see how Christ could die for all, how it was possible for Him to be Representative Man and both recognize and expiate the sins of humanity.

Others complain that they cannot understand the *effects* of His sacrifice, if it be intended to cover all our fallen race. Its effects on individuals they can grasp with the mind, and even share in experience. But all humanity——?

Let us be clear, first, that the Bible teaches that it was for the whole world that Christ died. 'God so loved the world that He gave His only begotten Son. . . .' All the 'Comfortable words' of the Communion Service are universals. 'Come unto me *all* ye that labour and are heavy laden and I will give you rest.' 'This is a faithful saying and worthy of *all* acceptation, that Christ Jesus came into the world to save sinners.' 'If *any* man sin, we have an Advocate with the Father, Jesus Christ the Righteous: and He is the propitiation for our sins.'

The unity and solidarity of the human race is a commonplace of modern thought. Real as individualism is, it is only half the truth of our human existence. Although we are persons with personal responsibility, we are bound to our race and family life in every part of our nature. From the shape of our nose to the idiosyncrasy of our temperament, we belong to others. The past of our people, and of the whole race, is in us. When God shared with man the joys of creation, and gave him the privilege of begetting children. He gave him the privilege of begetting *his kind*. The very strength of will with which some men assert their independence of all others is inherited from an ancestor who probably took a more modest view of himself and was grateful to the people who had gone before.

Human solidarity is real. We are, in large part, the past. Even the future does not come from the front to meet us, but streams up over our heads from the past, What we have done affects what we *will* do; what our forbears did affects as also.

Seeing that we gain so much by our place in the whole, we cannot complain too bitterly that we must bear the penalties of solidarity as well. Sin is the chief penalty. We come of tainted stock. Every human being is infected with sin. 'There is none righteous, no, not one.'

Christ came and shared our life. He did not abhor the virgin's womb, but begotten of the Holy Ghost, He was born without taint. Tempted at all points like as we are, He never sinned. Sharing our nature, He could stand in our place. Being without sin, He could see sin, and being without it, He could expiate it as well.

Moreover, when He wrestled with sin and defeated it, it was with the sin of the *whole world*. In all His dealings with persons, we see the alchemy of His indwelling working itself out, and foul men and women being made into shining saints. But again, this is only part of His triumph; in a sense, the smaller part. The central victory was the breaking of the evil principle of sin, the snatching of our whole race from sin's dominion. 'Be of good cheer,' He said to His disciples as He measured Himself to the Cross; 'I have overcome the world.'

Many people today, interested in social righteousness (and who is not?), are deeply impressed with socialized sin. Sin inheres, they truly say, in the very stem in which we live. Of course it does. The 'world' which is condemned in the New Testament is the world organized apart from God. The central primal sin is the assertion of the self against God. Of course, sin inheres in our whole system of life.

But it is the way of some social reformers to excuse man from all obligation for the situation as it is. They pity the 'masses', and talk much of the wrongs inflicted upon them. They are often less than frank with them about their sins.

No man is dealing adequately with the moral situation who makes it a matter of class distinction or racial difference. Sin infects *humanity*. It is in all the colours and all the classes. It is in the capitalists and the communists, the socialists and the conservatives, the democrats and the republicans, the nationalists, and the imperialists. That man is mentally and morally immature who over-simplifies the human dilemma, and sees the whole problem of wickedness in the group he dislikes. The problem is not a political theory, or a form of government, or what coloured rag blows over which bit of earth—but *sin*—sin which inheres in the whole race and in every member of it, in me as I write, and in you as you read.

In a way which no man claims fully to understand, Christ broke the power of sin in the Cross. He broke it in *principle*, and He broke it for the whole world. The fruit of the victory began to appear in the hour He was nailed to the wood. The dying thief responded—and where he led, all may come. Individuals illustrate the sublime outworking of the sacrifice, but it was offered for the race, and the sweep of this salvation encircles the whole world.

A British soldier came across the body of a Japanese officer in the jungle, and buried it. Then he put a cross on the grave. Telling his comrades later what he had done, he said: 'I don't know what the padre would think, but he said once in a sermon that Christ died for all, so I don't see how I've done wrong to mark the grave in that way. I suppose Christ had a thought for that poor beggar too.'

IX

What must I do if the Cross is to benefit me?
We set out in this chapter to discover how to get 'me' into the Cross, and our journey is almost at its end. Is it possible now to gather together the fruit of our thinking, and have a sense of utter security in this central citadel of our faith?

Let us go over the things which have become clear as we have travelled and thought.

The sins which nailed Christ to the wood were the same sins as I have committed. In that sense, I can truly and shamefully say that I have crucified the Son of God. I was there when they crucified my Lord.

It does not matter that fifty-seven generations separate my need from His provided succour. When I
knew the depth of my sin, I knew the provision of my
Saviour.

No martyr could save me. A sinful man could be a
martyr. Only a suffering God could save me from my
sin.

I certainly cannot save myself. There is sin even in
my good. There is something to be forgiven in the
best things I ever do. I am unsure of the purity of my
motives in the holiest moments I know.

Clearly, the Cross was necessary. Would God have
allowed it otherwise? My own blunted conscience has
point enough to tell me that sin must be punished or
expiated. How can I ever be grateful enough for His
expiation?

It would be wrong to pretend that I understand the
Cross even now. It outruns my reason, though I am
glad it does not contradict it. It seems to have meaning
even for worlds beyond this. I will seek to understand
it in every particle of my being, and yet not rest in my
understanding but in His deed.

I can see now why people make so much of the
blood of Christ. Could anything else speak in such
scarlet terms of His utter self-giving? The metaphor is
dearer than ever.

It is glorious to know that His sacrifice covers the
whole world. All may come. It is glorious to know that
the principle of sin has been broken, the central eter-

nal righteousness on which alone a righteous order can be reared is all secure.

What then must I do now?

I will go and sit before the Cross. I will *attend* to it. I will be concentrated, and unhurried, and let it speak to me.

> *I take, O Cross, Thy shadow,*
> *For my abiding place . . .*

Yes, I must *abide* here. Here is cleansing, security, and renewal. Here the past is dealt with, and the future secured, and all the present—peace. Here I take strength for service, patience in waiting, and healing for any wounds that come.

I rest my whole weight on the Saviour. I no longer care about myself. I do not need to. What freedom to be rid of all that fretting self-concern! In any case, *He* cares for me. As He teaches me, I will give all my care to others.

> *O safe and happy shelter!*
> *O refuge tried and sweet. . . !*

> *Beneath the Cross of Jesus*
> *I ever take my stand.*